Dr Andrew King

be bright
Living for Christ at University

"Andrew King has rammed it chock-a-block with good, sensible advice for new students"
— Michael Reeves

INCLUDES:
5 Part
Study Guide

DayOne

© Day One Publications 2013

First printed 2013

ISBN 978-1-84625-393-5

Published by Day One Publications
Ryelands Road, Leominster, HR6 8NZ

TEL 01568 613 740 FAX 01568 611 473

email—sales@dayone.co.uk

UK web site—www.dayone.co.uk

USA web site—www.dayonebookstore.com

Printed by Gomer Press/Lewis Printers

Dedication
This book is dedicated to my daughters Grace and Kerry. May you both grow up to live brightly for Christ whether you go to University or not.

CONTENTS

FOREWORD

The summer before I went up to university, a wise old Christian said to me 'As soon as you get there, find the Christian Union, get stuck in, and they'll help you find a good church.' It was great advice, and that's just what I did. In fact, I got stuck into loads: as well as my studies, I found wonderful friends, played a lot of sport, and drank mad amounts of coffee over chats about the meaning of life.

For me, the student years were a time of amazing fun, challenge, and opportunity. And I grew more than ever as a Christian. That was me. But I've also seen people really miss out and slip up. Particularly, I've seen Christian freshers so dazzled by all that's on offer that their love for Christ is slowly—and tragically—eclipsed.

The thing is, there's something uniquely special about the student years. As a student, there's more chance than ever to think about what you believe, who you are, and to start living how you want to live. And that means that, more than any other time of life, your student years will set the trajectory for what the rest of your life will look like. After graduation, work, mortgages and the rest usually mean that people just run along the path they've already set for themselves.

That's why this little book is a good one to read. Andrew King has rammed it chock-a-block with good, sensible advice for new students. It will help you think through the practical things (like how to study), as well as the deeper issues (like knowing who you are). And that will mean helping you to grab these precious years and make the most of them.

So enjoy the read, have a brilliant time at uni, and may you shine like a star as you live and speak for Jesus there!

Michael Reeves

INTRODUCTION

I know your time is precious so can I begin by thanking you for setting out to read this book. Although I suggest you read each chapter in one go, you may find it better to put the book down between chapters and have a pause. Hopefully you'll find my approach helpful but I expect you'll benefit from revisiting parts of the book again to weigh up my reasoning.

You're probably reading this because you're on your way or already at university. But if you are still undecided on whether to go please turn to the back and read the Appendix "Why go?"

But for those of you starting out at university: will it be a good thing for you? Will it be a great maturing process, a time of spiritual growth and evangelism? Or will it be a time of overwhelming worldly influence, compromise and drifting from Christ? Well, it should and can be the former—a good time to grow spiritually and to proclaim Christ well. Can I encourage you that your time at university can be a wonderfully enriching experience?

But there are very real dangers to be avoided. I want your days at university to be amongst the best of your life. Why shouldn't you be used by Christ to do great things for him? Why shouldn't Christ use your witness to bring many other young people to faith? My days at university (and I went to three different universities to study three different degrees!) were fantastic. I want yours to be even better. My aim is equip you so that you thoroughly enjoy your time at university whilst serving Christ.

Youth is a time for dreaming. Amongst all the day-to-day activities at university, don't lose time to sit back and question what you are learning and what is going on in the world. You need to think about why you do things and about the content of your course. Your studies are meant to provoke you to ask big questions and to challenge the status quo. Universities have historically been the birthplace of radical, even revolutionary ideas. Political and social change have often developed from student debates, which have fired up generations to bring great change. Some of these revolutions have been based on ideals of justice and freedom.

In the West much recent change has come from more selfish desires to promote ungodly ideas of moral freedom and the right to do wrong. But why should it stay like this? As a Christian, you not only have a radical message to tell, but you also have a powerful God to help you. The apostle Paul saw the need for this type of radical thinking when he said, *"Do not be conformed to this world, but be transformed by the renewal of your mind"* (Romans 12:2). Whatever you are studying, ask big questions about why things are as they are. Is your subject heavily based on humanist thinking? Then how can you work with others to carefully challenge and even slowly change this? Science, history, geography, and anthropology—the list is almost endless. What about the social issues that dominate our lives? Ethics, feminism, sexuality, poverty, debt, consumerism, the environment? You have a wonderful opportunity to serve Christ through your studies by applying biblical principles to the various ideas and challenges of your subject. Isn't that exciting?

Jesus teaches us that we Christians *are* the salt of the earth. In fact we are the *only* true light of the world (Matthew 5:13–16). Perhaps like no other time of your life, at university you will have both the time and the environment to engage in truly radical Christian thinking. Think of all the ways as a Christian that you would like to change yourself and the world. Use your time well. Get a grip of the Bible and study it book by book. Aim to read it all and set time aside to pray over what you read. You could start informal research groups to share ideas and gather new material to inform your thinking. You could set up debates with other students to promote a wider discussion.

University can and should be a great experience. Don't see your time as just a means to an end. Make it your goal at university to glorify Christ. I hope this book will help you flourish and "be bright". Sure, bright academically through hard study; but also bright spiritually by living a distinctively Christ-centred life. Rumour has it that some atheists are now claiming to be bright. May the joy and love of Christ in you enable you to shine brighter and even warm some of the cynical and hostile folks you encounter.

BE BRIGHT

I hope you eventually make it to the end of the book. More than that, I hope your journey through the book stimulates and informs you with good biblical ways to "be bright" at university. If it does do that, I urge you to recommend it to your friends as well.

I'd love to hear what you think. Have I missed a point? Do you want me to say more on something? Then please do get in touch: bebright@inbox.com.

Warmly in Christ,

Dr Andrew King

FURTHER READING:

Harris, Alex & Brett, *Do Hard Things.* Colorado Springs, Multnomah, 2008.
Stott, John, *The Radical Disciple.* Leicester, IVP, 2010.

PART 1: Before you go

WHO ARE YOU?

What is your worldview? Well, firstly let me explain what a worldview is by comparing it with your far smaller bedroom-view. Imagine you are lying on your back on the bed in your bedroom. Now, tell me where the window is: on the right, left, ahead or behind you? What about the door? What about the wardrobe? As you read this you are, no doubt, able to picture in your "mind's eye" where all these things are. That is your bedroom-view and you carry it around with you wherever you go. Now a worldview is similar in that it is a picture you also carry around in your "mind's eye" about the orientation of the big questions of life: Who am I? Why am I here? Why do I struggle? Who can rescue me? etc.

So, who are you? Identity is important for a number of reasons but principally because who we are shapes how we live; whether consciously or not, we all live out of our assumed identity.

The Bible explains that most basically you are a person created in God's image; it teaches that in Genesis 1:27 *"God created man in his own image, in the image of God he created him; male and female he created them."* And so your true identity will always be bound up in your relationship with God: how that plays out in your life will have a bigger impact than anything else. You were made to know and enjoy the loving relationship that the eternal Father, Son and Holy Spirit generously and graciously gives.

But it is blindingly obvious to us all that this is not the day-to-day reality in our world; most people do not live enjoying the loving relationship that the eternal Father, Son and Holy Spirit generously and graciously gives. Instead, their identity and yours has been profoundly shaped by your ancestor Adam who gambled everything by turning away from God with the desire to become his own boss. Don't merely blame him though, because you too have willingly joined that rebellion and naturally preferred your own rule to God's. So who are you? You are someone who has spurned the love and fellowship of the God who made you. The Bible calls this sin, and pronounces that as more than just messing everything up—your sin has evoked God's righteous anger.

The apostle Paul explains that *"the wrath of God is revealed from heaven against all ungodliness and unrighteousness of men, who by their unrighteousness suppress the truth"* (Romans 1:18). And so your sin and rebellion has earned you both death and judgement. It explains why the world (including your world) is in such a mess; it explains why so many horrible things happen and why so many things just don't add up; it explains why many of the things you hope for are dashed; it explains why many of your pet projects (even your education) can become all consuming yet remain unfulfilling.

All the above is most certainly true of you. But my more pressing question is whether your identity has remained in Adam and his rebellion. Or has your identity radically changed from that to now being in Christ? I am writing this book to Christians but I want you to pause and consider whether this includes you.

You weren't born a Christian; that myth is deeply held in many Western cultures on the premise that you "have to be born something" so you are either born a Muslim, Hindu, etc or Christian. That is such a deadly lie. Yes, you were born something: you were born a rebel. Yes, that rebellion may have been "cleaned up" by following an organised religion like "Christianity". But that has not made you a Christian. No one is born a Christian!

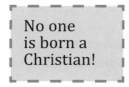

No one is born a Christian!

Instead, Christians are people originally from any number of "religious" or "non-religious" backgrounds who have turned from despising and rejecting God's love to valuing and welcoming it. At the heart of this change was a profound and sober acceptance of their sin and guilt before God. Whilst initially leading them to despair, this will have also led them to hear and believe the wonderful gospel news: God has provided a Saviour to rescue them. The gospel message is that God has come to us, as promised, and taken our place. Jesus is God the Saviour and his death on the Roman cross around 2,000 years ago was the promised event that would save a vast number of people from their sins. It was the

death of a holy and innocent man who swapped places with the people he promised to save. On the cross Jesus took the sinner's place.

And a Christian is someone who has realised they need to be saved and has entrusted himself or herself to the Saviour whom God has declared to have sent. And, being profoundly shaken and comforted by this news, a Christian then starts a new life (so radical that it is called being born again) as a willing follower of Jesus.

But does that describe you? Is your identity now in Christ rather than in Adam? Do you know, love and serve Jesus as your Lord and Master? When the apostle Paul wrote to people in a church in Corinth he challenged them on this: *"Examine yourselves, to see whether you are in the faith. Test yourselves"* (2 Corinthians 13:5).

Who are you? Are you being remade into the image of Christ? Whereas your ambition was once only to please yourself, now it is to please him and live for him. Do you pray to him, seek to obey him and, above all, love and enjoy his wonderful love and fellowship?

If you have experienced this radical, life changing conversion then praise God! You're a Christian, a new person with a new identity in Christ. The apostle Paul teaches that *"... if anyone is in Christ, he is a new creation. The old has passed away; behold, the new has come"* (2 Corinthians 5:17). That is amazing! But it doesn't mean everything has changed all at once. Your new life will continue to be a struggle; but a struggle that, by the Holy Spirit, you are guaranteed to win. The apostle Peter says in 1 Peter 5:8, "*Be sober-minded; be watchful. Your adversary the devil prowls around like a roaring lion, seeking someone to devour.*" What does he suggest we do to protect ourselves? He calls us to resist the devil. Paul tells us to put on Christian armour so that we can withstand the devil's attacks (Ephesians 6:10–18).

But what if your identity is not in Christ? What if you know nothing of your sins being forgiven and a new life started? Then I urge you to find out more about Jesus Christ and to repent and believe in him and you will be saved (Acts 16:31). Please get help now (you can contact me if you wish at bebright@inbox.com).

HOW PREPARED ARE YOU?

No one expects to finish a marathon if they don't do any training. What can you do (if you've still got the time) to better prepare yourself for university? After all, three plus years is quite a long time! I want you to think through three different areas of preparation: decisions, time and money.

DECISIONS

Our modern culture talks up the importance of individual freedom and champions the idea that we are free to do as we please. And so one clear temptation to you as a young Christian student is the notion that "you are now a free agent". Of course it may well be tempered with the recognition that your parents were trying to help. It is just that they set the boundaries far too close and don't appreciate that things are different nowadays.

At university you will be making many more decisions than you ever have before. But you must resist the notion that making the same decisions as your parents and home church leaders somehow makes you a clone. God doesn't want you to take that view. Far from giving you parents to cause you trouble, he has provided parents and local church leaders to care for you and to teach you how to make wise decisions.

Our modern culture will tell you that parents' and church's views are old and outdated. But the Bible teaches us that parents have been given to guide, protect and equip us for a life that pleases God. Instead of throwing it all away, thank God for all this instruction and hold onto it. This is what God says to us in Proverbs 6:20–22: *"My son, keep your father's commandment, and forsake not your mother's teaching. Bind them on your heart always; tie them around your neck. When you walk, they will lead you; when you lie down, they will watch over you; and when you awake, they will talk with you."*

Hopefully over the years your parents will have taught you from God's Word and increasingly gave you the space to make decisions yourself. What if your parents haven't taught you from God's Word but more from their own church tradition or personal preferences? Well, notice the caveat that God has wisely given in Ephesians 6:1, where he says: *"Children, obey your parents in the Lord, for this is right."* As a young adult away from home you are fully entitled to—and should want—a biblical explanation for the instructions your parents give. You are to obey them "in the Lord", that is, according to the Bible. If they cannot give you a biblical reason then you are not bound by such over-demanding views. God has also wisely given us freedom of conscience on finer matters of detail (see 1 Corinthians 10:23–33) to further guard against any abuses of parental or church authority.

But the main point here is that you are still to keep hold of your parents' and church's teaching where they agree with the Bible. They have no "best before date" on them. Rather, their teaching is there to guard and guide you through the rest of your life. Now that is radical—to show you love the Lord by keeping your father's commands! That is the witness your unbelieving friends desperately need to see.

So you are to make decisions *yourself* at university: you are a young adult. But please resist the notion that making the same decisions as your parents make is necessarily weak. Remember that your identity is now in Christ and you are to be renewing your mind by God's Word. If your parents made decisions after studying God's Word then it stands to reason that you will be drawn to make similar decisions. And if you are not sure about something, why not ask for advice from mature Christians you trust?

> Resist the notion that making the same decisions as your parents make is necessarily weak.

Yes, on some things you may see things differently; but always strive to have God's Word as the basis for your thinking, and not the godless culture around you.

TIME

I once asked one of my students who was hopelessly disorganised how he ever managed to pass his A levels. His secret ingredient had been his mum! She reminded him what homework he had, packed his bag each day, and even told him which classes he had! But he did not have his mum with him at university.

You will have to manage your own time and make

tough decisions about what to do. So, on top of all your study time, you will need to manage your social time (which really means limiting your social time to allow for study time) and your day-to-day cleaning and, possibly, cooking time. Most importantly, you will need to organise your daily devotional time and regular church time. Whilst this may all seem very obvious, this aspect of university life is far from easy when two or more things are competing for the same time slot. A common short-term solution is to stay up later in the evening to fit everything in. However, few students thrive with continuous late nights, insufficient sleep and irregular study patterns.

So how prepared are you to manage your own time? Well that depends on whether you are currently relying on your parents to manage your time for you. What happens when you are left to your own devices? What happens at weekends? How often do you need other people to remind you to do something? If you are poor at this then you need to develop coping strategies such as a diary, calendar on your laptop or mobile phone. Remember, no one else will do this for you at university.

Another important thing is to get into a routine now. Now I know routines can be taken to an extreme. I heard of one student who optimised the route of every single journey and daily event to save time and effort. That would drive me mad. Yet it is a good idea to set days of the week when you will stay in and work. At least then you can let your friends know so they don't interrupt you with tempting offers of coffee and chats. You can then make sure you are able to get your studies done, socialise <u>and</u> attend Bible studies and prayer meetings. Whilst certain weeks may not be possible, good planning should allow you to make Church/CU attendance the norm.

The argument that you will be too busy to attend church is weak. Very few of us find it hard to do the things we really want to do. A pattern of non-attendance is likely to leave you spiritually malnourished.

MONEY

Another obvious area that needs suitable planning is money. This is particularly relevant in the current climate as tuition fees and student debt look set to be here to stay for some time. Over-spending on a tight budget can be all too easy. Part-time work can help but this needs to be carefully thought through so that it does not cause other problems. So, before some practical application, what are the biblical principles students should apply to this important subject of money?

You need to plan out a realistic budget of all your costs: accommodation, food, books, clothes, travel, socialising etc—and stick to it! If you just spend money without any limits or thought for future bills, it will not be long before you overstretch your funds and stress yourself. As you will probably have a "lump sum" at the start of each year you might find it helpful to open a savings account and in-effect pay yourself each month so that you have a fixed amount of money to deal with a month at a time. In this way, you may more practically avoid eating into future resources, rather than overspending at the beginning and trying to skimp on everything at the end of each term.

As with time management, money management is a skill learned over time. If at all possible, develop a responsibility for your own money now. Perhaps your parents can give you a monthly allowance (based on how much it costs them already) to let you practise budgeting and keeping your cash! Even as a student you should see the principle of sharing as one that applies to you. Whilst this clearly applies to supporting the Lord's work financially in some way, it also applies to our possessions, our hospitality and our own free time. If you really want to serve God in this way, you won't be legalistically arguing what the minimum amount is to give of this and that. If you are, you have missed the point. It's not the amount you give, it's the way you give. The apostle Paul reminds us that *"God loves a cheerful giver"* (2 Corinthians 9:7).

But above all, learn to be content. You may meet some financially rich students who will try to make you look inadequate. Remember that your heavenly Father supplies all your needs, and that your life is more than the sum of all your belongings. You have Christ and he is the pearl of greatest price. Make sure you treasure him most of all and learn to be content with the things he has chosen to give you. Even at university you can show how much you love and value him by not living for, or loving money most of all.

CONCLUSION

In project management there is a saying that *"failure to prepare is to prepare for failure"*. Whilst that might sound a little dramatic, the principle does carry over into everyday life. And so, the best way to thrive at university is to be prepared beforehand by already having good habits. First and foremost you must turn from your rebellion and run to Christ! But you also need to get in the habit of managing your own life: making your own decisions, arranging your own time and managing your own money well.

FURTHER READING:

Beynon, Graham, *Mirror, Mirror.* Nottingham, IVP, 2008.

Chandler, Matt, *The Explicit Gospel.* Nottingham, IVP, 2012.

Greear, J D, *Stop asking Jesus into your Heart.* Nashville, Broadman & Holman, 2013.

Hall, John, *Christian Basics.* London, Grace Publications Trust, 2009.

Hughes, Barbara, *Disciplines of a Godly Woman.* Wheaton, Crossway, 2006.

Hughes, R Kent, *Disciplines of a Godly Man.* Wheaton, Crossway 2006.

Strobel, Lee, *The Case for Christ.* Grand Rapids, Zondervan, 1998.

STUDY QUESTIONS
Part 1: Before you go

1. Why is the idea that "Christianity is just something you are culturally born into" so wrong and so dangerous?

2. Who, according to the Bible, is a genuine Christian? What is the sole basis for a person being assured of forgiveness of sin and eternal life?

3. What are the core ambitions of a genuine Christian? Do you share these?

4. At university you will be making many more decisions than you did before. What new decisions are you making?

5. Time and money are always under great pressure. Discuss what strategies you can develop to use these precious resources well.

6. Youth is a time for dreaming. What big ideas and hopes do you have for your time at university?

PART 2: Living for Christ

Well done! You're either on your way or already at university. Now what? How can you make any impact on the mass of humanity around you? Hardly anyone has even noticed you exist, let alone come asking for your pearls of wisdom. What does "living for Christ" mean anyway? Would anyone notice even if you did? You know I am going to remind you that Christ will know. And what a motivation that is. But you'll be surprised at how many other people will also be looking you up and down. And never forget the lasting joy that is found in serving Christ.

BE HOLY

One of the most important things to do is to start well. Each academic year kicks off with a non-teaching "fresher's week". It is designed to help new students (the freshers) settle in. During the week you are expected to digest a near impossible amount of information. You will get introductions to your accommodation, and the mandatory list of do´s and don'ts. Then there will be tours of university buildings and facilities like the library, health centre and student union. You'll meet the main staff associated with your degree programme and have some introductory lectures/seminars to break-the-ice with your student group. If by the end of all this you can remember which building you are in and find your way back to your hall then you will have achieved something. Everyone knows there is an awful lot to take in; but it is important for you to attend this so you can start the first week of teaching knowing what to do.

But aside from the business side of fresher's week, there will also be plenty of time and opportunity to socialise: most universities will hype up these events to excite you, and attract students to study in their particular town or city. The night life, clubs and bars will be well advertised and you'll receive a number of discount offers and persuasions not to be the odd-one-out who stays behind in their room. And after the night out comes the customary kebab, followed by a trip to the off-licence and then on to the party at so-and-so's flat. With many young people and lots of alcohol, the expectation of many students is to "get wasted" and more.

Holiness has never had a good press. In fact the nickname "Puritan" was scornfully given to Christians who were passionate about being pure, about being holy. Perhaps you shudder to think that many of your theological ancestors were Puritans? Well, I expect a few were rather po-faced, but from their literature we see that they lived very vibrant, warm, active and fulfilling lives. They loved music, art, games, and fun—but all done to the glory of God! Sadly, many Christians view the Puritans through the twisted and cynical writings of non-Christians.

Yet "to be holy" is the clear calling of every Christian! How we manage to doubt this is amazing; yet we all have to fight the temptation to rationalise away the need to be holy. Just consider the teaching from the apostle Peter: *"As obedient children, do not be conformed to the passions of your former ignorance, but as he who called you is holy, you also be holy in all your conduct, since it is written, 'You shall be holy, for I am holy.' And if you call on him as Father who judges impartially according to each one's deeds, conduct yourselves with fear throughout the time of your exile, knowing that you were ransomed from the futile ways inherited from your forefathers, not with perishable things such as silver or gold, but with the precious blood of Christ, like that of a lamb without blemish or spot"* (1 Peter 1:14–19).

Peter argues the necessity for holiness from a number of angles. Firstly, he makes the central point that we are to be holy because God is. We thought earlier about how we are all made in God's image and therefore we are to image holiness. And now, as children adopted into his family—just think of it—we shall want to take on the family likeness. Of course our big problem has been sin but that, in itself, proves the priority of holiness. As sin (unholiness) is our biggest problem, how can we ever rationalise away the need to be holy? Secondly, Peter teaches that our prior unholiness displayed our ignorance, but now we have come to Christ and seen the glorious light of his holy nature: how could we choose darkness again? We have been truly enlightened. We have been made bright. So, be bright! Thirdly, Peter reminds us of the awesome price our unholiness cost Christ—his own precious blood. We must regularly remind ourselves that Christ himself "bore our sins in his body on the tree." Our passion for holiness shows our grateful thanks for his sacrifice to save us.

> Holiness is vital. So why do we so easily devalue its importance?

Holiness is vital. So why do we so easily devalue its importance? Why can we so often rationalise living in ways which (when we dare to be honest) we know are against God's Word and therefore unholy? How can we imagine that the Holy Spirit (exactly, the *Holy* Spirit) is not grieved when we conform to the passions of our former ignorance?

AVOID LEGALISM

We are saved by grace—free grace, amazing grace and nothing but grace. But there are other people who aren't saved who imagine their endless keeping of rules will please God, but it won't. And there are some people who are saved by grace who, nonetheless, still think that being saved, now they need to work hard to show that they are saved. Won't a passion for holiness look like legalism?

Well, let's be clear: we are only saved by Christ's finished work on the cross as a gracious gift to those who receive it by faith. Strictly speaking we are not saved by faith (as if faith on its own were any good)! Rather, it is that Christ fully accomplished our redemption on the cross. But it is applied to us through God's gracious gift of faith. And just as becoming a Christian was only possible because of divine intervention, so being a Christian is only possible by God's Spirit.

Yet why have we been saved? The Bible is clear that it is more than merely to be "saved from" Hell. Praise God we are forgiven and given a new life! But that new life is a new life in Christ; it is a new life where we live like Christ and not like Adam! Remember, your identity is now in Christ. And so what does that mean? It means that you are full of love for Him. That is the proper motivation for holiness.

Not working hard to look saved, but loving deeply such that we strongly desire to become more like the one whom we love. And what is the process of becoming like Christ called? It is called sanctification, which is another term for "becoming holy".

So will a passion for holiness look like legalism? Not if it is motivated by a deep love for Christ. Legalism has the nasty tendency of wanting people to look at ourselves—"Just look how good I am doing." Yet love for Christ will have the wonderful effect of making us want people to look at Christ instead. As you desire to be transformed into the image of Christ—who is perfectly holy—so you will want people to be drawn to him.

The deadly thing about legalism is that it is another form of self-worship. Remember the Pharisee who was so pleased with his "holy life"? He prayed, *"God, I thank you that I am not like other men, extortioners, unjust, adulterers, or even like this tax collector. I fast twice a week; I give tithes of all that I get"* (Luke 18:11–12). He wanted a pat on his back; he wanted God and others to praise him. But when we love Christ more than anyone else, when we surrender all to him then we are motivated by worship of him, not ourselves in our obedience. It is because we want to be like him and are so grateful for his sacrificial love that we are passionate for holiness. Can that look like legalism? Perhaps it can from a distance, but closer up it will look like love.

When Paul was teaching Christians living in Ephesus, he urged them *"do not grieve the Holy Spirit"*

(Ephesians 4:30) and went on to warn them *"sexual immorality and impurity or covetousness must not even be named among you, as is proper among saints. Let there be no filthiness nor foolish talk nor coarse joking, which are out of place, but instead let there be thanksgiving"* (Ephesians 5:3–4). During your time at university this kind of behaviour may be all around you, yet you are called to keep well away from this and rather be passionate about growing more like Christ.

Yet before we move on to other things, please do also see the more positive aspect of holiness: it makes us suitable for God to use. You can quickly see the need of sterilisation when it comes to surgical equipment used in an operating theatre. Who would want to have an operation with contaminated tools? Similarly, holiness makes us suitable for God to use in his kingdom. Remember, he is holy and therefore he separates us to himself so that he can then use us as instruments in his hands. What an awesome calling! When you, out of a deep love

> Holiness makes us suitable for God to use in his kingdom.

of Christ and through the inner working of the Spirit, live a holy life you are clean and ready for God to use to bless others and glorify his name. Wow! Be holy.

DAILY DEVOTION

How can you cultivate holy living? By having daily devotions. What I write now I write directly out of my own experience: for many years I have struggled with regular daily devotions yet I urge you to keep working towards (or keeping alive) a pattern of time daily in the scriptures/a good devotional book and prayer. Of course we are all busy and find routines hard to follow. Yet most of us manage some form of routine each day. So why do some of us find daily devotions so hard? Well, it is true that the Christian life is a spiritual battle and every distraction will seem more worthy of your time. But I expect two other problems also exist.

Firstly, pride is and always is my biggest problem. Why oh why do I so quickly assume that I can live today without Christ? Why oh why do I so readily believe that I can still honour him without needing a fresh supply of his saving grace and life-giving Spirit? It is because my pride fools me into thinking I am who I am not. I urge you to see your own pride and self-reliance and to repent of it. Without Christ we are nothing and each day we depend on him entirely if we are to truly honour him.

Secondly, devotion is more than study. I think the failure to see this has also reduced my success in keeping regular devotions going. Too often I have approached the Bible or a devotional book as a mere intellectual puzzle to solve: what new insight am I going to find today? Yet, although that may stretch my mind, it is unlikely to warm my heart. I would argue that central to healthy daily devotions is time delighting in Christ. Sure, at other times it is good to stretch our minds and plumb the depths of teaching contained in God's holy book. But in order to increase love, in order to stir a passion for holiness we must focus on Christ. When I slowly came to see this, I did two things differently: first I reduced the quantity I attempted to read (and spent more time reflecting on the truth of those words) and secondly I turned back to older writers (such as the Puritans) where, despite some flowery language, I found food that warmed my heart more than stretched my mind. You just may find this adjustment helps you, particularly if, like me, you are a more analytical type.

MAKE GODLY FRIENDS

Yet although you should have a passion for Christ that leads to a passion for holiness, you must still develop and enjoy human relationships. The notion that you need to seclude yourself in your room to be holy is not only daft but dangerous. It is daft because the Bible repeatedly teaches that our hearts are where holiness must begin. Alone in your room you can very easily disappear into a world of unholiness, with or without the help of the internet. But it is also dangerous because your identity in Christ is an identity with community. Our eternal God is an eternal community of Father, Son and Holy Spirit. And so, being made in his image, it is not surprising that we are fundamentally social people.

Our heavenly Father is not unrealistic. He knows you intimately and knows that you are a social creature. The idea of "shutting yourself off in your room" should seem odd because it is. You have been created by God to want to make friends and enjoy their company. And so the answer to this problem lies in the type of friends you make. You need to make godly friends. Many of those friendships will last for the rest of your life and will prove to be an immense blessing.

So how will you meet and make godly friends? Well an obvious way is to get involved in your university's Christian Union (CU). Details of this should be easy to find on the Internet otherwise contact an umbrella organisation (in the UK it is called UCCF). Many Christians will naturally find their way to the CU and, hopefully, you will find other folk who are passionate about loving and following Christ.

Yet there is another, perhaps more natural way. Simply don't hide the fact that you're a Christian. If an opportunity comes up to show you are a Christian, take it! Not only will other people know where you stand, you will probably help encourage other Christians to speak of their own faith as well.

Never let the aim of making friends lead to a compromise with ungodliness. Paul reminds us in Titus 2:11–12 that *"the grace of God has appeared, bringing salvation for all people, training us to renounce ungodliness and worldly passions, and to live self-controlled, upright, and godly lives in the present age"*. Now of course this doesn't mean you should have only Christian friends or that you need to launch into a 5-point sermon with each of your non-Christian friends! But it does mean you need to "be open" about being a Christian. If you're not, you will not only be stressed by the situations that confront you, you will spoil your witness and dishonour God. The best way to stay on track is to have a strong group of godly friends. Your Christian brothers and sisters will not only help you have fun in a way that glorifies God, they will also help to equip and strengthen you as you also form strong friendships with unbelievers.

JOIN A LOCAL CHURCH

A few years ago a friend planning to go away to study explained she was deciding between two universities. She asked for some advice, so I looked up the local churches and suggested she went to her second choice. Her first choice university was in a rural setting and the closest evangelical church was a 20-mile car journey away. Whilst it had a perfectly good course, she wouldn't be able to attend a church there because there was no public transport to it and she had no car. However, she went to her first choice. A few months later we learnt she wasn't attending that church or any other. So it didn't surprise us that when Christmas came she didn't come back to her home church. The temptations of worldly friends were too great and without the practical means, soon church attendance and Christian living became things of the past.

Of course that's just one case. But the important practical point you must grasp is that although you will be away from your home church, you must not treat university as a time when you can be away from all church. And although godly friends at university can be a huge blessing, you must not allow them to become your surrogate church either.

Sadly our individualistic culture makes it harder to prioritise a real commitment to a local church. And with the busyness of student study and social life the discipline of setting aside the time for church life is hard. Yet church community life is fundamental to being a Christian.

A local church is not merely a "Spiritual Accident & Emergency" ward that just needs to be there for when you have a crisis. Of course, the brothers and sisters in a local church will seek to help and support you through any crisis, but that isn't the main reason for church. Nor is church a "Spiritual Top-up Point" ready to give you a top-up on a Sunday morning for the rest of the week. Of course, the preaching and teaching ministries of a local church ought to feed your soul but hopefully it isn't a mere preaching station. If preaching were all that we needed then you would be justified to "go to church on YouTube". Why settle for a second rate local preacher when you can hear the best in the world?

The Bible, however, repeatedly speaks of Christ's followers as "a people", a gathered number of people who then share their life (of worship, learning and serving) in the location God has put them. One of the best descriptions of a local church is as a family—sharing life together. A family is dysfunctional if everyone simply raids the fridge and then eats alone! A family is dysfunctional if they live in the same house but barely spend any time interacting.

Next in importance to finding a course of study that really suits you, is finding a local church that can become your new family for the years of your studies. It really is that important. Because you will need a place that you can call home, somewhere you can make genuine attachments to new brothers and sisters in Christ. Yes, you will probably receive plenty of student lunches and home cooking! But far more than that, you will receive counsel and support, a place of accountability and (catch this) somewhere you can also serve.

Your time at university ought not to be a three year sabbatical from Christian service. Your youth, energy and ideas can be a vital ingredient to enrich and develop the life of your student local church.

BELONG

The early Christians described in Acts 2:42 *"devoted themselves to the apostles' doctrine and the fellowship, to the breaking of bread and to prayers."* Each of these aspects of church life needs to continue with you in your life as a student. Remember, your identity is to be found in Christ, not in your studies or your social life. The writer to the Hebrews also teaches you that you should *"not [be] neglecting to meet together, as is the habit of some, but encouraging one another, and all the more as you see the Day drawing near"* (Hebrews 10:25).

> Your identity is to be found in Christ, not in your studies or your social life.

I remember someone challenging me on the need to be committed to a local church: *"I'm committed to Jesus Christ, that's what matters! I am devoted to him … Not any ragtag group of Christians!"* Did he have a point? No! Because when we are truly devoted to Christ, we are also devoted to what he is devoted to. And who is Christ devoted to? His bride. His church! And so we are to be devoted to a local church ... because he is.

Let me quote the veteran preacher John Stott: *"If the church is central to God's purpose as seen in both history and the gospel, it must surely also be central to our lives. How can we take lightly what God takes so seriously? How dare we push to the circumference what God has placed at the centre?"* In fact, the 1st century Jerusalem church practise is all the more striking given that many of them had come to Jerusalem on a religious holiday and so probably didn't see themselves as long-termers. They were much more like university students! Yet they devoted themselves to the life of this new church for the time they were there.

Can I urge you to make this one of your ambitions while you are at university? To be devoted to local church teaching (to know the full counsel of God); to be devoted to fellowship (to live shared lives with the other members); to be devoted to the breaking of bread (having both the Lord's death and his coming back regularly on your mind); and prayer (not just individual, but collective prayer as you call out together for the Lord's help).

Joining a local church can bring you many blessings. An obvious one is the regular teaching from God's Word which is vital if you are both to deepen your understanding and also to feed your soul. Yet there are other blessings too. The local accountability to the members and leaders can be a great protection against slipping away. If you remain on the fringe of a few churches you will easily be able to stay under the radar. But is this wise? Joining a church gives leaders your permission to look out for you and challenge you if needed. Don't be too proud or independent not to see the blessing this can be. Dive in and enjoy the community life Christ has saved you for.

A local church can also help root you in the wider world in contrast to the restricted focus of the young student world in which you will be spending most of your time. It's good to regularly be amongst older and younger people, amongst those from a variety of different backgrounds.

BIG OR SMALL?

Many university towns and cities have churches that become known as "student churches". These are often big churches with solid Bible teaching and vibrant student support ministries. For many students these churches are an immense blessing and are more attractive places to invite friends.

But do also remember the smaller churches that will often exist in the same area. I write as a pastor in a small Baptist church and so freely confess my vested interest here! Often a small group of enthusiastic and committed students can be a huge blessing to a smaller congregation. As already mentioned, do remember to see your time at university as a time of serving as well as being served. Might the smaller church (perhaps even closer to you) be a place you can serve Christ?

Smaller churches can be small for a variety of reasons: some good and some bad. Perhaps they have failed to properly adapt as time has moved on; perhaps they simply lack the gifts to be more "professional"; perhaps they hold to particular doctrinal teachings that are less common. But perhaps they are too easily overlooked for the larger more comfortable student churches? Might you and some of your friends be able to be a great blessing to the smaller number of godly folk in that decidedly non-student church?

FURTHER READING:

Beynon, Graham, *God's new community.* Nottingham, IVP, 2010.

Chester, Tim & Steve Timmis, *Everyday church.* Nottingham, IVP, 2011.

Dever, Mark, *The Church: The Gospel made Visible.* Nashville, B&H Publishing Group, 2012.

DeYoung, Kevin, *The Hole in our Holiness.* Wheaton, Crossway, 2012.

Harris, Joshua, *Why church matters.* Colorado Springs, Multnomah, 2011.

Ryle, J C, *Holiness.* Darlington, Evangelical Press, 2010.

Tullian Tchividjian, *Unfashionable.* Colorado Springs, Multnomah, 2012.

STUDY QUESTIONS
Part 2: Living for Christ

1. Holiness has never had a good press. Why is this? What wrong thinking leads some Christians to see it as a chore?

2. What are the two extremes to Christian behaviour? What can you do to avoid them both?

3. Why is it so important to have a good network of Christian friends?

4. Why is the notion of the "lone ranger" Christian so common? What makes some Christians want to remain isolated?

5. John Stott wrote: "If the church is central to God's purpose as seen both in history and the gospel, it must surely also be central to our lives." Discuss the reasons church is not always seen like this.

6. What are the advantages and disadvantages of being part of a smaller local church?

PART 3: Studying for Christ

WHY ARE YOU STUDYING?

Of course there will be a whole host of surface reasons for why you are studying: you love the subject (hopefully), you are excited about a career in this field, you sense both the opportunity and the ability etc.

But I am asking a deeper question. What is your deeper motivation and goal for your studies? You may be tempted to answer "to glorify Christ of course ... " and to skip on to the next section. But can I urge you to stay with me and read through this section?

The issue I am getting at is identity. Just who do you see yourself as in the deepest sense? Many people find their identity in something that they see as strong or positive about themselves. Perhaps they turn heads because of their looks; perhaps they have trophies on their mantelpiece that speak of sporting achievements; perhaps they have good connections. For many people what they do becomes their identity. Where they work or, for folks more like you, where or what they study. Their identity is in their studies and that can be a dangerous thing for you as well. How can you tell where your identity is? Let me give you two simple tests:

1. What do you like to talk about? When you meet someone new, what are you longing to tell them? Where do you steer the conversation? That is probably where your identity is.

2. What do you spend your extra time on? All of us

have flexible time in which we can choose what we do. What do you default to doing? That is probably also where your identity is.

And so there is a real danger that "being a university student" can become your identity. If it does you are in great danger. Seriously! I want to explain three reasons why this would be dangerous:

1. YOUR STUDIES MUST NOT BECOME YOUR GOD

You and I are in a never ending war of worship. Will we worship the true and living Father, Son and Spirit or will we construct a substitute god to worship? And that struggle does not stop when we "become Christians". The pull toward idolatry—having a substitute god—is as real for a church leader as it is for anyone else. Believe me, your studies can easily become your god. And if they do you will find your identity and purpose in the pursuit of them.

Yet each Christian has his or her identity in Jesus Christ. It is being in him that truly defines who they are. It is living out of the settled identity as an adopted brother or sister of Christ that is a Christian's true identity. Whilst you should study hard, and do a full week's study you must fight not to allow them to take over. They will do if you find your comfort and identity in talking about them, more than you do in talking about Christ. They will do if being known for your studies or place of study is more significant to you than being an adopted brother or sister of Christ. Is Christ your Lord and Saviour? Or are you seeking day-to-day salvation and self-worth from your study programme?

Sadly the pull of idolatry is almost as old as the hills. Right from the beginning of time, mankind has looked for satisfaction in the creation rather than the Creator. The theologian John Calvin rightly observed that our hearts are perpetual idol factories that manufacture man-made alternatives to finding our satisfaction and identity in worshipping the true and living Father, Son and Spirit. It was true of many of the Israelites in the Old Testament days. Jeremiah the prophet was told by God, *"My people have committed two evils: they have forsaken me, the fountain of living waters, and hewed out cisterns for themselves, broken cisterns that can hold no water"* (Jeremiah 2:13). Did you notice that it was God's people doing this? Or, to bring it up-to-date—Bible believing, evangelical Christian students today can commit two evils by forsaking Christ as their main satisfaction and identity and turning to their studies instead. What a disaster! Compared to the Lord Jesus Christ even the best studies in the best university leading to the top grades is like a broken cistern that holds no water. Your studies must not become your god.

2. YOUR STUDIES MUST NOT EAT ALL YOUR TIME
Of course, if they do become godlike to you then they will demand more and more of your time. Sadly this is a far too common mistake for Christian students to make. Their thinking starts off well: I want to do well and not be lazy like some others. But before long the healthy

desire for hard work can morph into an unhealthy obsession to achieve and achieve and achieve.

The Lord has built into a healthy life a balance of work, rest and play. The Lord has called each of his people to prioritise time within the church community and, especially, to keep the first day of the week separate from general work. You will have to establish good habits and maintain strict discipline if you are to stop your studies from eating all your time.

> The Lord has built into a healthy life a balance of work, rest and play.

But can it be done? Is it reasonable to expect students these days to restrict study time? Isn't it all different nowadays? Well much has changed, but the abiding principle of putting God first certainly hasn't! In my experience, time off from studies made study time more effective. And time with the Lord's people and in his Word was always a better long-term blessing.

3. YOUR STUDIES MUST NOT DEFINE YOUR FRIENDS

Not everyone goes to university. And as a Christian you must therefore work hard not to slip into an assumed elite of those who do. Back home you will have family and friends outside of higher education. Hopefully in your local church whilst at university you will also have a variety of friends as well.

Do work hard to make sure that your studies do not begin to define your friends. If you do you will be denying the gospel's ability to bridge all man-made barriers. Whilst sin separates us into different classes and pecking orders, the gospel teaches us that with our identity in Christ all barriers can be broken down. But your studies can become a very real barrier; some people carry a sense of inadequacy or regret that they didn't follow a path to university.

So I urge you to be intentional in keeping your studies as just a part of your life. Don't let them slowly become your identity, source of meaning and therefore worship.

Study to learn new things; study to grow in your understanding of more of God's great wonders; study to think his thoughts after him. Study to push forward the boundaries of understanding in your subject area and to do great things for your fellow mankind. But, above all, study to know Christ better and to enjoy living out your new identity in him.

FURTHER READING

Beale, G K, *We become what we worship.* Nottingham, IVP, 2008.
Beynon, Graham, *Mirror, Mirror.* Nottingham IVP, 2008.
Keller, Timothy, *Counterfeit gods.* London, Hodder & Stoughton, 2010.

YOUR ORGANISING TEXT

As you undertake your studies—in whatever subject or field—you are likely to soon face the challenge of authority. When conflicting ideas are evident, to what should you turn? Where is the ultimate authority that ought to shape everything else you think and do, to shape your worldview?

Well, the Bible is our ultimate authority. Yet whilst that can be relatively easy to agree with in principle, it is vitally important that you understand just what that actually means. And, because I believe it is so crucial that you get this clear in your head, I am going to spend some time developing my point.

My point is that the Bible, and the Bible alone, has all the major organising principles you will need to orientate your thinking as you approach the myriad of challenges and puzzles in your subject. No, I am not saying a few proof-text verses will solve your equations. No, I am not saying that your subject is directly referred to in the Bible. But I am saying that the Bible provides all the major organising principles you will need to allow you to construct a God-honouring framework in which to wrestle with the challenges you will face. The Bible alone must be your ultimate "organising text".

Am I suggesting you stop reading other books? Not at all—keep reading this one and many more. Am I suggesting you only read books that support a biblical worldview? No, not that either. So what am I saying? I am saying you must view all sources of information like individual mountains in a vast mountain range. And as you do that, you must see that the Bible is the Mount Everest of all mountains by far. It is the highest, most lofty book of all and you must view all others from its perspective. The Bible must shape and form your worldview so that you organise everything around its words——and not automatically the words taught by your Professor.

Have you scaled literature's Mount Everest? Have you spent time exploring its various facets and the complex shape of scripture? Do you return frequently to sharpen your perspective on other peaks? Have you viewed Mount Biology or Mount Psychology from the viewpoint of scripture?

Sadly many students go to university confessing to be "Bible believing Christians" only to find the challenge from other sources overwhelming. By spending far too much time in other sources, the authority and sufficiency of scripture gets eroded until they become practically agnostic about the real use of the Bible outside of their church walls. Yet a Bible that "only works" within the walls of a church is about as useful as a chocolate teapot! And so students who begin to organise their outside lives according to another text, slowly slide into a thoroughly secular mindset.

To help you see that the Bible really ought to shape *everything* you think and do, I want you to see three pillars of truth: the Bible is God's revelation; it is God's accurate revelation; and it is God's sufficient revelation.

REVELATION

Writing to a Christian called Timothy, the apostle Paul wrote that: "*All Scripture is breathed out by God*" (2 Timothy 3:16). Older Bible translations use the word "inspiration" but this can be misleading. It was not that God gave visions and dreams that inspired men to write—like an artist might see a landscape and be inspired to paint. No, Paul is teaching that the words recorded in the Bible have themselves been breathed out by God. And so "breathing out" emphasises their exact origin. When you speak to a friend, the ideas that start in your head are turned into movements in your mouth such that you breathe out ... and form words. And in the same fashion, God the Spirit has breathed out his Word.

Whilst sometimes I might have a reasonable idea what is "on your mind", most of the time I will remain in the dark unless you reveal it to me. And that is what Paul is teaching of the Bible: it is God's revelation of his mind! How else would we know these things? Perhaps we might have discovered evidence for what God has done, or found eye-witnesses. But we do not need to, because God has revealed his mind and left us the written record in his book.

Now it is also perfectly true that the Bible is also full of the authentic words of men: *they* thought them and *they* wrote them. And yet Peter explains, "*No prophecy was ever produced by the will of man, but men spoke from God as they were carried along by the Holy Spirit*"

(2 Peter 1:21). God, who is sovereign in every detail of life, so arranged even the background, character and situation of these men so that their authentically human words had their origin in the mind of God.

Think about it. We have in the Bible the mind of God! And so Paul urges us to hold on to the scriptures because they are the very word of God.

The scriptures are the word of God; the 66 books received as scripture are equally and fully God's Word and carry full and lasting authority. Yet a common view today holds that whilst the New Testament might be God's Word, surely we cannot believe that of the Old Testament as well? Isn't the Old Testament, with its Creation and Fall account, and other dramatic events just a fanciful myth? No!

Jesus Christ—the main character of the New Testament—viewed the Old Testament as God's Revelation. When speaking to the Pharisees Jesus said, *"You leave the commandment of God and hold to the tradition of men"* (Mark 7:8); and when discussing the question of resurrection he referred to the book of Moses saying, *"Have you not read in the book of Moses, in the passage about the bush, how God spoke to him, saying, 'I am the God of Abraham, and the God of Isaac, and the God of Jacob?'"* (Mark 12:26). Each time, Jesus referred to the Old Testament words as being from God.

Repeatedly Jesus referred to the characters and events recorded in the scriptures as historically true. He considered God to be the real maker of mankind and in such a way that its truthfulness upheld his argument about divorce and marriage (if God as creator is a myth then what authority do his commands to his mythical creation have?). He viewed Abel as historically real and referred both to Noah and the flood as historical facts when he said, *"Just as it was in the days of Noah, so will it be in the days of the Son of Man. They were eating and drinking and marrying and being given in marriage, until the day when Noah entered the ark, and the flood came and destroyed them all"* (Luke 17:26–27).

> A biblical worldview that is only based on part of the Bible will be incomplete.

So what does that mean for your studies? It means that as both old and new testaments form the Bible you must read, study, believe and absorb the teaching of all of it. A biblical worldview that is only based on part of the Bible will be incomplete.

ACCURATE

So God revealed his mind in a series of writings which were written between 1500 BC and 100 AD. But are the translations we have today still accurate? Ought we to still use them as our organising text now that more recent writings sound more convincing? Can you see how this turns the pressure up? How can we claim such old writings are still worth believing?

We do well to remember that many principles of modern life are still based on ancient texts. Despite our western culture's obsession with modernity, most of the maths we do is still based on the principles recorded by people like Euclid and Pythagoras! Why? Because none of it has been proved wrong! Unless someone can prove that the 66 books of the Bible are false or inaccurate we Christians ought not to lose our confidence in them!

The "Chinese whisper" theory sounds credible until we consider the facts. This common idea suggests that the Bible we read today is the product of thousands of retellings that have introduced profound errors. Yet we have available to us literally thousands of ancient manuscripts, some from as far back as the 1st century AD, that match up with astonishing accuracy! And these manuscripts are well attested to be genuine!

Imagine actually playing Chinese whispers with a hundred different rows of a hundred people. The same initial message was whispered along each row and then the last person in each row was asked to state their message. Now, if all one hundred of those last people all had the same message ... with only trivial differences ... would you have more confidence in the message? You would, wouldn't you! (And you'd probably conclude that some supernatural supervision was going on as well.) Well that is the empirical accuracy of the Bible today.

But even if it is the same book, how can we be sure it started out accurately? Wasn't it from the start a powerful mix of fact and fiction? Well again, one of the most helpful things to see is the viewpoint that Jesus had on the accuracy of the Bible. Jesus' view of scripture as historically true is important (he believed in an historical Adam, used the teaching in Genesis as a basis for his teaching on marriage, and believed Jonah was swallowed by a great fish). Indeed, by referring to the more miraculous and least acceptable events (according to critics) as factual history, he asserted his view that it was unimpeachable. And because he upheld that scripture is truthful in its historical claims, he upheld that all other scripture can be considered reliable and true, including teachings about the reality of sin and the predictions about his mission to come to save sinners.

But why am I pressing the point that the whole Bible is accurate? Well let me tell you a story to illustrate my point. One day a farmer noticed that someone had been stealing the pumpkins out of his field. What could he do to stop them? He went back with a sign to scare the thieves. It said *"Warning: one of these pumpkins has been poisoned!"* But the next morning the farmer was surprised to see a second sign next to his. It said *"Warning: two of these pumpkins have been poisoned!"* Do you see? Even if the farmer had poisoned one pumpkin, at least he knew which one it was. But now: he had no idea if another one had been poisoned and, if so, which one! The whole crop was ruined. And it's the same when people want to remove awkward parts of the Bible today. If that bit is myth, what about this bit?

We must see that precisely because it is God's

revelation it is also accurate—all of it. And so it is imperative that you stand firm to the Bible and use it to shape your worldview. I know, that isn't easy. In the final analysis I believe the Bible is accurate because I believe it is God's revelation. But there is strong empirical evidence to help support this as well.

SUFFICIENT

As you undertake your studies—in whatever subject— you must allow the Bible to be your "organising text" from which you view all others. Why? We have seen that it is God's accurate revelation of himself. But is that enough? Can't a book be accurate but incomplete?

Well yes, a book can be 100% accurate but incomplete. But—and here is a vital point—the Bible itself claims to be sufficient for us. Let me quote the apostle Paul's words to Timothy: *"All scripture is breathed out by God and profitable for teaching, for reproof, for correction, and for training in righteousness, that the man of God may be complete, equipped for every good work"* (2 Timothy 3:16–17). Now here's the vital point: we have already seen that the Bible is accurate and so when it claims to be sufficient that must be an accurate claim. Praise God! We Christians have all that we need for the various aspects of life.

Does that mean that we don't need to study other books? Not at all. Earlier on I encouraged you to read, read, read other books. But we must see that all other texts are sub-ordinate to the Bible. The principles and teaching contained in the Bible are authoritative and binding over every subject and issue you study at university.

Although Jesus performed many miracles, his view of scripture was so high that he claimed it was more powerful than his miracles. In the account of the rich man and Lazarus, the rich man asked Abraham to send him back to earth to warn his brothers. Yet Jesus records Abraham as saying, *"'They have Moses and the Prophets; let them hear them.' And he said, 'No, father Abraham, but if someone goes to them from the dead, they will repent.' He said to him, 'If they do not hear Moses and the Prophets, neither will they be convinced if someone should rise from the dead'"* (Luke 16:29–31). This suggests Jesus viewed scripture as the ultimate authority; even signs and wonders have a lower authority to God's abiding Word.

So how should this affect your studies? It ought to shape all of them! Of course that doesn't mean every subject will be shaped in the same way, but all of our thinking ought to be brought captive to obey Christ (2 Corinthians 10:5). What the Bible teaches about identity, sexuality, purpose, authority, worship, etc. all impact on the subjects you will study at university.

Will the principles all be obvious? Not at all. But you are at university to study and think hard, and as a Christian you have both the responsibility and the privilege of mining God's Word to bring out deep and wise principles to shape your area of study. What a fascinating task. As Johannes Kepler is credited as saying first: whatever you discover, you will only be thinking God's thoughts after him.

As you study for Christ at university, I urge you to make the Bible your organising text. It is God's revelation to you and it is accurate and sufficient to orientate your study in any academic discipline. Sure, you will need to study many other books too, but you must synthesise them with scripture, not the other way around.

Given that we are all still affected by sin, we must see that whenever our understanding or our desires are out of step with scripture, it must be we who are wrong. We cannot claim to be guided by fresh teaching from the Spirit as he will never contradict what he has already written. We should see therefore that we are powerless to understand the Bible without the Holy Spirit. You must pray earnestly that the Holy Spirit will give you understanding of the word and skill to apply it to your field of study. Without the application of the Spirit to the word, you will not develop a truly Christian mind.

Apparently there is a car bumper sticker in the USA which reads *"God says it, that settles it"*. Is that what you believe? I do hope so.

FURTHER READING:

Edwards, Brian, *Nothing but the truth*. Darlington, Evangelical Press, 2005.

Edwards, Brian, *Why 27?* Darlington, Evangelical Press, 2007.

Kistler, Don (ed), *Sola scriptura*. Morgan, Soli Deo Gloria Publications, 2000.

Pearcey, Nancy, *Total Truth*. Wheaton, Crossway, 2008.

White, James, *Scripture alone*. Bloomington, Bethany House, 2004.

YOUR WORLDVIEW

What then is a biblical worldview? What corner pieces should you have firmly set in place as you set out on your university studies? Through what framework of understanding ought you to analyse the entire scope of existence?

Well, clearly I am not going to exhaust this subject here. But I hope I can help you see the major elements of a biblical worldview that will enable you to study in a way that honours the Lord Jesus Christ.

ELEMENT 1: GOD IS AT THE CENTRE

It starts with a big bang! The Bible opens with the dramatic opening line ... *"In the beginning, God ..."* (Genesis 1:1). That is the big bang of scripture. What a start! No warm up, no justifications or explanations. Genesis begins by revealing our great & majestic God!

Do you, before you talk to someone, give them various proofs that you <u>are</u> indeed there? So why should God? Obviously he believes there is enough evidence already without him needing to begin Genesis 1v1 with a philosophical, moral, and metaphysical proof that he does in fact exist!

"In the beginning, God ..." This must be the foundational piece of your worldview. Everything else is based on this! It is called monotheism: mono meaning one, and theism meaning a personal God.

So what are the alternatives?

- **Polytheism** has a shop window full of gods: you

pick and choose the one that suits you.

- **Henotheism** allows you to pick one god as yours although others are valid. This is called pluralism today.
- **Pantheism** attempts to soak god into the universe and make everything god. This is very popular today ... with the so-called green environmental movement.
- **Deism** has one god of creation but who has "wound the universe up like a mechanical clock" and now left us to get on with life by ourselves.
- **Atheism** just gets rid of the notion of God altogether because he is deemed impossible because someone or something *must* have created him!
- **Agnosticism** argues that we simply cannot (or at least currently do not) know. Whilst it may sound humble, very few agnostics do much to verify their position.

Depending on whom you are talking with, you will probably find one of these alternative foundational pieces in their worldview.

Must we choose? Need we choose? Perhaps you've heard the (essentially) postmodern story that defends this worldview? It refers to several blind men trying to describe an elephant. One felt the tail and reported that an elephant is thin like a snake. Another felt a leg and claimed it was thick like a tree. Another touched its side and said the elephant was a wall. And so, it is said, we are like these blind men, each having a limited view of god and so the various world religions only understand part of God, while no one can truly see the whole picture. We each have "part of the picture" so must not claim others are wrong. That would be arrogant!

It's a fascinating story but it has a massive flaw as an argument for pluralism. You see, the story *only* makes sense if the narrator has seen the *whole* elephant. For someone to claim that all religions are seeing just part of god they must have seen it all. They are actually claiming the very knowledge they say no one else has. That's incoherent!

Within western society atheism is by far the most common default worldview. Apologists for this view claim that a god cannot exist because he would also need a creator. Yet this too is incoherent.

If we ask an atheist whether she exists she is likely to agree. And the universe? She'll likely agree it also exists. And so when we ask what made the universe she is likely to trace things back to some infinitesimally small particle and an infinitely large explosion. But who or what made that infinitesimally small particle?

You see, either with God ... or with the particle ... you have to stop somewhere. I love the story of a little old lady who challenged a speaker following a lecture on astronomy and the solar system. "Your lecture is all wrong." she said "The earth is really a flat plate supported on the back of a giant tortoise." "So what is the tortoise standing on?" the lecturer asked with a superior smile. "On the back of another tortoise," she replied. "And what is *that* tortoise standing on?" pressed the lecturer. It was the lady's turn to be scornful: "It's tortoises all the way down!"

Whatever worldview people have, it has to finally rest on something, or someone! And so atheism's main claim against monotheism is itself incoherent!

> Atheism's main claim against monotheism is itself incoherent.

So how does God himself explain his existence? Who made him? Well he gave perhaps the most profound explanation to Moses at the burning bush. The bush itself was an explanation because it kept burning without being consumed: it was everlasting. And when Moses asked God who he was we read in Exodus 3v14 *"God said to Moses, I AM WHO I AM. This is what you are to say to the Israelites: 'I AM has sent me to you.'"*

Who am I? I AM. I have no beginning and no end. I AM! No one made God because he is the Eternal One! And that is the awesome foundational grandeur of the biblical worldview. In the beginning, before the beginning, was God.

There is nothing illogical about that claim: as God is the greatest being then the greatest attribute of that being is *self-existence*! The official name for this doctrine is the Aseity of God. It's a Latin word meaning

"from himself". We cannot fully get our heads around that—because we aren't expected to. That's the point. That's part of the wonder of thinking about God. He simply *is*!

Have you understood this? Have you been gripped by the awesomeness of this truth? God is God because he eternally is. No one, nothing is greater than him: no one or nothing gives him life. The buck truly does stop with him!

Nicolaus Copernicus was an Italian astronomer who lived in the 16th century. He is remembered because he challenged the long-held assumption that the sun revolved around the earth. [By the way, the idea that the "church" was the source of the geocentric view is nonsense. The church simply went along with the far older assumption made by the pagan philosopher Aristotle that the sun revolved around the earth.]

But the Copernican revolution literally transformed our view of the natural world! Yet the sad irony is that today millions of people who know about Copernicus desperately need the spiritual equivalent of his revolution! Because the personal, Trinitarian God of the Bible is at the centre. And he must always be at the centre of all your life too.

ELEMENT 2: GOD MADE IT ALL

After revealing himself, God proceeds in the opening verses of the Bible to stamp his design and ownership on all of the universe he made. We read, *"In the beginning, God created the heavens and the earth"*

(Genesis 1:1) yet too often we lose the sheer wonder of this revelation.

I once heard the fictional tale of God setting a one-week challenge to a group of top engineers and scientists. The challenge was to design and create a machine that can walk 50 yards unaided. They reckoned they could do it. So God set the clock ticking. On the third day God came to see how they were doing. They had their design drawings finished and were beginning to cut and shape different materials. *"Hey, that's cheating!"* God said to them *"They're mine, you are using my materials. You must create your own raw materials!"* The point of the tale was to remind us that even the raw materials we creatively use are still those God originally made!

Because the Bible reveals that God created *ex nihilo* (from nothing) in six days (and given his awesome power I take them to be literally days of 24 hours as the text suggests). Ex nihilo: things being created from nothing, not evolving over billions of years. Now that is awesome! And that is supernatural! God—who is all powerful—spoke and created a world that all belongs to him.

We saw in the last section that there are many worldviews even though there is only one world! So how can you tell which is true? The answer is by coherence—the true worldview will best fit together both with itself and with your experience of real life.

The main "alternative" to the biblical worldview

of origins you will encounter at university is called Naturalism: the view that Supernaturalism (the agency of One above natural things) is at best unnecessary and at worst impossible. This view asserts that the Cosmos has come into existence without the need of a Creator. This is the view of Secular Humanism (which governs much scientific thinking today) and neo-Marxism (which governs much psychological and educational thinking today).

How can you continue to hold to the Bible's claim of a Creation ex-nihilo by a personal God in such a hostile university environment? How can you be sure you are not committing intellectual suicide (or at best intellectual bigotry) in affirming such a minority view? Can you be an authentic academic and still believe the Bible? Well, it will take deep thinking but I offer the following observations to help you grapple with this challenge.

1. The beginning is an extraordinary event! Truly a "one off"!

We Christians need to be more confident here. Whether biblical six-day creation or naturalistic evolution is being discussed both are claiming to explain an extraordinary one-off event. And so we shouldn't be surprised if the language, if the format, if the explanation is different from how we explain other things. Launch events are (by definition) one-off events. And so the choice of words for explaining Creation in the Bible is likely to appear unique. An extraordinary explanation is not automatically historically unreal. Just consider the extraordinary explanation of naturalistic evolution!

2. Science actually means knowledge

Today the word science has a limited meaning—limited to just natural science (physics, chemistry, biology, astronomy, etc). Yet our English word science comes from the Latin word *scientia* which simply means knowledge. And so history is truly part of science because it deals with the knowledge gathered from eye-witness evidence (from which we get most of history). Incidentally, theology used to be called the "queen of the sciences" because it dealt with the most important knowledge—of God himself!

Our modern use of the word science deals with the very important work of suggesting theories and drawing conclusions from experiments made from repeatable events (such as an experiment in a laboratory). However, history deals with the equally important work of suggesting theories and drawing conclusions from gathered eye-witness and archaeological evidence from the past. The big difference is that modern science deals with the repeatable; history does not.

Why is this important? Because the Bible claims to be God's revelation of history. Don't believe the modern notion that Natural Scientists are the High Priests of all knowledge. Remember that there is more true knowledge than the stuff men in white lab coats tell us! We shouldn't expect to find all the answers confirming

6 days lying around in archaeology or through everyday empirical natural sciences. It is a category error! The study of repeatable physical events is called physical science; but the study of one-off events is called history.

Oxford Professor, John Lennox in his very helpful book *God's undertaker: has science buried God?* gives an amusing illustration. He described himself taking a cake to be analysed by a meeting of the world's top scientists. "Please explain the cake," he asked. The nutrition scientists told him about its calories; the biochemists told him about structure of the proteins and fats; the physicists told him about the different particles and how they bonded together.

"But *why* was the cake made?" John asked. Despite all their expertise and analysis, they couldn't answer. "*Who* made the cake?" he asked. Again, no answer. And then (to John's great surprise) his Aunt Matilda stood up, and *revealed,* "I made the cake ... and I made it for your birthday!"

Now, because the world is God's work we can study and analyse it, like a cake. But it is only God's Word that reveals who made it and that he made it to show forth his glory.

3. Micro evolution is not the same as Macro evolution

Most of you will have heard of Darwin's finches. Charles Darwin on his famous voyage in the ship called HMS Beagle travelled to the Galapagos Islands near Ecuador. He measured the features of birds living there (finches) including their beaks. However, when he visited other islands he noticed beaks were different. When back in London he developed the sensible idea that as the climate changed so the finches' beaks had evolved to suit the different climate and the need to scavenge for food. Great: all well and good.

But what the Naturalists don't tell you is that scientists today on the Galapagos islands are observing rapid changes in the finch beaks between large and small over a period of a year or two. Not one way traffic—but small to large to small again! This is micro-evolution. We see it all the time. In the United Kingdom we wear thick clothes and woolly hats in the winter. Come summer (we hope) to be in short sleeves with sun hats. We adapt too!

So it is vital that you understand that many with the Naturalist worldview claim that evidence for micro evolution can be seamlessly extended to macro-evolution. They assert that because a finch's beak evolved into different shapes, so finches also evolved into entirely *different* creatures (mysteriously leaving some of its brothers behind to remain as finches). But there is no evidence at all for that proposition! No one has ever seen monkeys evolve into humans being nor found a continuous trail of fossil evidence. Those holding to the Naturalist worldview simply insist it must have happened given the probability over enough time. [However the notion of irreducible complexity is a strong counter argument that it isn't even theoretically possible for such change however much time is allowed! Do see my recommended reading for more on that.]

It is vital that you understand that micro evolution (often reversible) is <u>not</u> the same as macro evolution from amoeba to man. Yes, there is evidence for the former; no, there isn't evidence for the latter.

4. Uniformitarianism is simply an assumption

Of course it is one thing to debate ideas and theories; it is another thing altogether to ignore tangible empirical evidence. And so one significant question affecting worldview concerns fossils. Doesn't the ancient fossil record simply torpedo the historicity of Genesis 1? Well, ask almost any palaeontologist (someone who studies fossils) and they will tell you that the interpretation of fossils rests on an assumption made years ago by a man named Charles Lyle. He asserted that the way things change today are

> It is one thing to debate ideas and theories; it is another thing altogether to ignore tangible empirical evidence.

(broadly speaking) the same as they changed years ago. That is, there is a uniform pattern of change over time. So, if today we observe that a new tree ring develops over 20 years and then we chop another tree and find it has 20 rings we assume it is 400 years old.

But whilst that certainly does explain many things, it is merely an assumption to hold that it explains all things. We have no strong evidence to support this "uniformitarian" view that all changes have evolved over millions of years of gradual change. In fact, we have some strong evidence against that assumption.

In 1980 Mt St Helens, a volcano in Washington State, USA erupted with many scientists as eye witnesses. These scientists had carefully observed the areas around the volcano before the eruption and then went back many years later (when it was safe) and recorded what they observed. They saw rock strata that weren't there a few years ago which looked (according to uniformitarian theory) to have taken millions of years to have formed. They saw trees fossilised in the rock which weren't there a few years ago which looked (according to uniformitarian theory) to have taken millions of years to have formed. They also observed rapid erosion and the rapid formation of new islands.

So there is evidence that things that *look* like they took millions of years to develop by uniformitarian change only took 20 or so years to change after a catastrophic event. And as the Bible teaches a universal flood—*the possibility should at least be considered* that the flood accounts for fossils and rock strata etc. Does this disprove uniformitarianism? No, but it does prove it is not a watertight framework for interpreting fossils.

BUT DO WE HAVE TO CHOOSE?

Can we have God and evolution? Some Christians say "yes" and hold to what is called "Theistic Evolution" where God is claimed to have *used* evolution to bring the rich diversity of life.

I believe that view leads to huge theological problems and should be resisted. Firstly, the notion of a single historical Adam is almost impossible to harmonise. When did the ape become man? Did all mankind descend from him or from other creatures? In addition to this, the concept of evolution requires the presence of suffering and death to allow progress. Only after billions of years of death is man said to have arrived on the scene. But the Bible speaks of an initially good creation with the intrusion of death as a punishment for the historical Adam's sin.

Paul boldly asserts in Romans 5:12, *"Therefore, just as sin came into the world through one man, and death through sin, and so death spread to all men because all sinned ..."* Here the Bible clearly teaches that sin is the cause of death. Death is not natural—it is a horrible unnatural curse, brought about because of human sin: *"sin came into the world through one man."* And Paul clarifies in v14, *"Yet death reigned from Adam ..."* A real man Adam sinned, and death started then. However, the theistic evolution view has to allow God to use millions and millions of deaths ... both plants, animals and evolving humans ... before creation is complete.

And, to my mind at least, that contradicts God's word. No, macro-evolution is not in a biblical worldview.

ELEMENT 3: WE ARE UNIQUE

God is at the centre of everything and he made it. But

the third element comes closer to home because it is about the worldview we should have of ourselves. Just who are we and how ought we to relate to God, to each other and to the rest of the cosmos?

The biblical worldview is that mankind was made separately from the animals. Human beings have not evolved from apes, we have been made distinctly in God's own image. The author of Genesis states "*So God created man in his own image, in the image of God he created him; male and female he created them*" (Genesis 1:27). This is sometimes called the *Imago Dei*: image of God in the Latin language.

Why don't we go to the vet when we are sick? Because we are not animals! According to the Bible mankind's closest relative is not a monkey, but God himself. And having this view securely in your mind is crucial as you come to many areas of study at university. It will radically change the way you see solutions to human problems. So what are implications of understanding that all human beings are made in the image of God?

1. We have dignity
Our dignity is not "man made" to give us a feeling of worth! No, we are made in God's image and whatever society says we have dignity. This explains why murder is so wrong! To murder is to attack the very image of God. Killing another human being is hugely different from killing an animal because humans image God himself. And that includes abortion and euthanasia.

Human beings are not to be ordered around or disposed of at the wish of the more powerful! It is a scandal that the most dangerous place for a human being to be today is in the womb! In England & Wales around six hundred tiny babies are murdered every day.

Not all, but some working in the field of eugenics look to the evolutionary theory of "the survival of the fittest" to justify getting rid of the disabled, getting rid of those with genetic defects. Yet every human being has inalienable dignity because he or she is made in God's own image. If God in his infinite wisdom allows such situations to arise, our response is to be that of love and care—not brutal disregard and distance.

Now it is at this point that I want to show you the point of great inner conflict many naturalists have. We have seen that there are many worldviews on offer but only one world. How do we determine which is true? We look to see which is internally coherent and matches the empirical evidence around us.

So when we ask why mankind has dignity (and let's be clear most people sincerely *do* believe this) we need to find a basis for this view. The biblical view upholds a high view of human beings because of our identity in God's image. But if we are merely advanced apes we face a great struggle stopping a creeping pragmatism on who or what deserves dignity. If an unwanted unborn baby has none, why should it have any more outside the womb as a unwanted born baby? Surely we are free to develop new norms? Surely as financial and social pressures grow we will need to adopt a "survival of the fittest" framework? Now in their hearts most people find a great inner conflict here. Why? Because their operating worldview is in conflict with truths placed deep inside them by God.

As you undertake your studies at university you have a massive opportunity to gently raise these issues. But if you are unsure of the Bible's teaching (or sure yet frightened by the opposition) you will find yourself tacitly supporting the very opposite of what is true.

The fact is that, when pushed, the people who teach you and study with you need to see that on the point of dignity they are still operating with the light of God's image in them. Logically, their operating worldview gives them nothing but a "common consensus" view of dignity which means if the majority change their mind the weak and vulnerable have no hope.

2. We are creative

Our word culture means to cultivate: to develop, to make progress. Agriculture is doing this with the land and our general word culture means doing this with everything else. Right from the beginning of Creation, the Bible reveals culture and industry: *"Adah bore Jabal; he was the father of those who dwell in tents and have livestock. His brother's name was Jubal; he was the father of all those who play the lyre and pipe. Zillah also bore Tubal-cain; he was the forger of all instruments of bronze and iron"* (Genesis 4:20–22).

Why has industry and culture developed amongst

humans right from the first days? Why are we creative in a vastly different way than animals? Why indeed are you bothering to study and develop your field of interest at university? Because being creative is in our DNA. We are made in the image of *the* creative person—God! It's in our God-given make-up to create and develop, to innovate and progress. Not *ex nihilo*! We rely on God to supply the raw materials.

Birds still simply build the same nests (perfectly suited but fixed) as they always did. Pigs still scavenge for food and wallow in mud (unless factory farmed) as they always did. Yet look at human beings. We have developed. Why? We all have a quest for "progress" because we were made in our great God's image with the capacity to think, to speak, to create and ultimately to know him.

All of us have an in-built ability to create in the image of God. Maybe it's with art, music or literature. Or perhaps with cooking, clothes, materials or machines. Maybe it's taking an idea and putting it into practise or taking a group and building a team. Creativity comes from being in the image of God.

Again, this is a point where thoughtful naturalists have an inner conflict. How can they explain human creativity in clear distinction to the animals? Survival of the fittest? Then why haven't the plants and animals all died? Why are changes in the natural world so much smaller than the human world? Why do we long for (and establish) far more than "survival"? How can the support of "the arts" be truly justified?

And before they go romantic and talk of "living back with nature" ask them whether they also relish having no sanitation, healthcare or infrastructure?

3. We are relational

Why is loneliness so painful? Because God tells us it is not good: God designed us to be in community. He has made us in his image: the image of a relational eternal Father, Son and Spirit. We are relational at heart because our God is. "*Then the LORD God said, 'It is not good that the man should be alone; I will make him a helper fit for him'*" (Genesis 2:18). Relationships lie at what it is to be human! A biblical worldview reveals why healthy people have such a strong desire for company, for friendship and community! (No, not Facebook, but face to face!). And more intimately too: "*Therefore a man shall leave his father and his mother and hold fast to his wife, and they shall become one flesh*" (Genesis 2:24).

Isn't it marvellous that people from distant parts of the world are able to communicate and form relationships? People with vastly different external circumstances are still able to find ways of getting along. Why are we deeply concerned when we hear of people in need, even on the other side of the world?

Now, again, we must remember that there is only one world and only one true worldview. And so it is not surprising that many naturalists live with conflict within their formal worldview and their inner convictions. Yes, they do care about relationships (and it would be both dishonest and naïve to suggest they really don't: they do). But why? What basis do they have for the universal phenomena and value of deep human relationships?

The usual formal answer is that relationships have evolved as a coping strategy. We are said to have realised that cooperation aids survival. Well I am sure it does. But few of us are really satisfied with that explanation when it comes to our own relationships. A merely utilitarian view of life is deeply disturbing (we are relational only for what we can get out of others). It might sound fine in theory but the idea that I am only interested in you for my own gain will make you (rightly) feel abused! No, we long for deep and lasting relationships based on value and worth; not you scratch my back and I'll scratch yours!

Any of you that study humanities subjects or psychology, sociology, anthropology etc will find that the very nature of your studies is based on the notion of human relationships. With a biblical worldview you will be better equipped to show their deep, deep origins: deep in the very character of the Trinitarian, relational eternal Father, Son and Spirit.

4. We are responsible

Actions have consequences; most people will accept that. Even postmodernists who theorise that life has no meaning and there is no right or wrong will complain if you punch them on the nose! Yet the logic of a naturalist worldview cuts across what we all know and feel within.

A biblical worldview shows that God made us with a "will"—part of us that makes decisions about what we will and will not do! The first man Adam was made morally responsible. *"The LORD God took the man and put him in the Garden of Eden to work it and take care of it. And the LORD God commanded the man, 'You are free to eat from any tree in the garden; but you must not eat from the tree of the knowledge of good and evil, for when you eat of it you will surely die'"* (Genesis 2:15–17). He was simply told not to eat from one tree—and held responsible if he did.

Worldviews really do have consequences. So, if you hold to a naturalist, evolutionary worldview how do you justify the near universal concept of responsibility?

> Worldviews really do have consequences.

One popular view is to claim society has to enforce moral codes etc for "the good of the many". But who are the many? How are minorities protected? The hidden assumption is that the "State" is self-governing through some form of democracy so that all are protected. But does that mean the majority is always right?

Another popular view is to claim people are not ultimately responsible for their actions because they are victims of nature (their dysfunctional bodies) or nurture (their dysfunctional families). But is the paedophile or the mugger just sick? Ought prisons to be abolished? Such a view requires that approved intelligentsia need to re-train us to be free from the shackles of the past. We are not responsible for our actions because the past was enforced on us! But if we are all imprisoned by the past, how did the intelligentsia ever break free? How can they re-train us? A worldview without God, with "mere accidental animals struggling to find their own way" may sound free and easy—but it always causes conflict.

In your studies, you are almost always going to find the worldview of "who we are" cropping up in various theories and assumed solutions. We almost all believe other people should be held responsible for their actions (especially when they do wrong to us). Without a biblical understanding of mankind you will not be able to articulate a coherent reason for that reality.

ELEMENT 4: THE WORLD IS CURSED

Whatever a person's worldview they will accept that there are "things deeply wrong" with the world. In fact for some of you, the questions of "what is wrong" and "why?" will underpin all that you study. Only the deluded think life today is bliss! Yet only a biblical worldview can connect the reason things are so profoundly wrong to a logical cause. It reveals mankind's rebellion as the root cause of the problem; a problem that has led to God placing a curse over the entire world and so affecting all things. This is massive: just three chapters into the Bible and the plot takes an astonishing downward turn. Everything else in world history is played out in this context.

God gave Adam and Eve a test: will you trust me? Do you believe I am good? Fruit on one of the trees in a garden of trees was marked out not to be eaten. There is nothing at all to suggest it was a bigger tree, or had better looking fruit. No—it is just marked out as the one tree God told them not to eat from. But they did. They rebelled. They did not trust God and believe he was good. Instead they believed a lie: that God was holding something good from them. In their minds, God was to be dethroned ... and they were to be on their own throne. And since that day forward mankind has wanted to be his own boss.

Although God created us—in his image—to be godly, we have chosen to be ungodly. Of course this is not pleasant news (and so is commonly denied). But the truth is that we see so much empirical evidence of deep hostility, selfishness and evil that it really is a hard task to deny. What else explains the global wickedness and ungodliness in the world? Why is there daily news of crime, vandalism, violence, fear and pain? Why do we all see deep within ourselves times of selfishness, unkindness, pride and rebellion?

Our worldview must include this sobering assessment of reality. To ignore this is to ignore the most gigantic elephant in the room! And so I want to unpack some necessary truths we need to learn about human sin & rebellion.

1. Human sin affects the physical world
The Bible reveals the effect of sin on the wider world.

We read in Genesis 3:17–18, "*And to Adam he said,
'Because you have listened to the voice of your wife and
have eaten of the tree of which I commanded you, 'You
shall not eat of it,' cursed is the ground because of you;
in pain you shall eat of it all the days of your life; thorns
and thistles it shall bring forth for you; and you shall eat
the plants of the field.'*"

Many of you will study the natural world and that
will include some consideration of "environmental
concerns". Is this caused by mankind? Well, at its deepest
level the answer is most certainly yes. Not based on
how much carbon dioxide we emit, but on our rebellion
towards God. Earthquakes, tsunamis, droughts, plagues,
famine, etc. were not in God's original world. God cursed
the ground because of human sin.

God is ultimately behind global disasters! He uses
them for his ultimate purposes. What greater disaster
has there been so far than the global flood recorded in
Genesis 7? Sadly mankind has become so proud that we
think we can "save the planet". But praise be to God that
one man has come who, because of his heroic work, has
secured the remaking of all things to a new perfection.
In Romans 8:19–22 we read: "*The creation waits in eager
expectation for the sons of God to be revealed. For the
creation was subjected to frustration, not by its own choice,
but by the will of the one who subjected it, in hope that the
creation itself will be liberated from its bondage to decay
and brought into the glorious freedom of the children of
God. We know that the whole creation has been groaning as*

in the pains of childbirth right up to the present time."

God has cursed the whole of the physical world because of our sin. Now, for sure, this is a hard truth. We may recoil from the idea that God has cursed the world. Yet that is exactly what he has revealed in his book! Whilst it is certainly a hard truth, we must also see that through Jesus Christ he has established liberation from the original curse. This is why the gospel message is so massively good. Yes we are to study and work to care for the natural world. But we must make sure that our biblical worldview removes any idea that we can "save the world" by ourselves. Although that task is too big for us, it is not too big for God!

2. Human sin affects everything we do

This fact is both vital and frustrating. It is vital that your worldview understands that sin affects all people and even the way we all think. It is frustrating because this then means that "a fully biblical worldview" will never be perfectly lived out in this age. And that makes it easy for our opponents to point to our "own goals"!

The teaching underneath this worldview is called "Total depravity". It does not mean we are all as bad as we could be (lawless Somalia is worse than leafy Surrey). But it does mean that no part of our lives is ever 100% free from sin. Every day will include sin; every hour will include sin; even every good deed will include sin.

No one likes this truth. When we understand it we feel the pain of the accusation. The prophet Isaiah teaches that even our good deeds are riddled with sin:

"All of us have become like one who is unclean, and all our righteous acts are like filthy rags; we all shrivel up like a leaf, and like the wind our sins sweep us away" (Isaiah 64:6). If we wanted to translate "filthy rags" literally we would have to write "used sanitary products". Exactly.

And the result of this universal spread of sin is that it always separates. It separates us from God, from each other and even from ourselves. That's why people want to "imagine God away"—that's the real attraction of atheism! They would rather live in denial—pretend an eternal speck made the universe—than confront the God who is there.

And this also leads to the reality of guilt. Much inner turmoil, depression and despair is the result of a deep awareness that our rebellion has not only blighted our world but also landed us "guilty as charged" before a holy God.

And so in your studies, whenever you study people without including the grim reality of sin, you will only have a small part of the picture. Sin truly is the elephant in the room in the study of many university studies. Whilst you may not be able to openly articulate this, you must be fully aware of it so that you can avoid adopting anti-biblical solutions that evade the heart of the matter.

ELEMENT 5: CHRIST IS THE ANSWER

Many people who hold to a different worldview do acknowledge there are deep problems in the world. However phrased, the reality of pain and suffering are rarely denied within western cultures. In fact, because sin is so deep and complex, many different causes can be legitimately cited. Yet a huge gulf will appear when discussion is made about the answer.

The most common answer given is that people have to individually "discover their right path". This idea is expressed in a variety of ways but essentially boils down to "self-salvation". Look for the hero inside yourself! All other people can do is give suggestions and guidance but the main task is self-discovery. For many people this is expressed through education and work (which is why teachers are today's secular priests) but for some this is expressed through therapy and drugs leaving many trapped in a dependency culture.

But we Christians are people who have been shown the way. Jesus Christ is the Way, the Truth and the Life! He is the answer because our deepest need is forgiveness and new life. For that we need a God-appointed rescuer, a Messiah, a Saviour. And that is exactly who Jesus Christ is: the one who buys us back from our slavery to sin; the one who redeems. Oh what a wonderful truth this is! How amazing—God offers all who will come to Christ full forgiveness and new life.

Yet whilst "conversion" is vital we must not think all the change will happen in one day. Far from it. And that is why you and other Christians need to engage in academic study to apply the deep truths of scripture to the complex world of rehabilitation, transformation and change. But just how does "salvation and renewal" happen? What is the biblical worldview on the massive topic of change?

1. Christ saves, we can't

Just the sheer scale of the problem ought to alert us to the fact that we are in too far. All of us are too far gone to expect self-recovery. No, redemption is entirely God's gracious work—from start to finish.

Throughout the Bible God is always seen as showing the initiative and working "behind the scenes" to bring about a recovery. Right back in Genesis after sin enters the world, Adam didn't say, "We will turn back, we will repent, we will not repeat this." Instead, sin multiplied. By chapter six sin is rampant, society is in a huge mess. Even after the global flood, the next generation at Babel returned to the same level of rebellion!

Yet God took the initiative and did the work to bring about *his* redemption. Did anyone expect God to use well over 2,000 years of time to bring about his plan of redemption? Throughout the Old Testament the cry kept going up "How long O Lord?" God's work of redemption was according to God's timetable.

The apostle Paul teaches that "*... at just the right time, when we were still powerless, Christ died for the ungodly*" (Romans 5:6). Why didn't Jesus come straightaway? Because that wasn't God's plan. Why doesn't Jesus come and totally transform you or me overnight? Because that isn't his plan.

Redemption is entirely God's work and he will do so according to his timetable. At times this is incredibly hard to accept: when other people are scorning the pathetic state of many local churches; when the credibility of "the church" seems to be blown away by scandal and division; when the gaping holes in your life damage Christ's reputation.

But you must hold firmly to this biblical worldview. Redemption is entirely God's work. Just as his timetable involved thousands of years passing before the Messiah came—so his timetable involves much patience today as he unfolds his purposes. Even your faithful witness at university—courageously holding to these biblical worldview elements—is his work.

2. Christ saves all sorts of people

A very popular idea you will come across at university is that Christianity is "just for white middle-class Anglo Saxons". It may well be expressed in different language but the concept of a niche religion for a particular cultural group is common. Yet as we review the biblical worldview we have been assembling, we can see how incoherent the idea of "niche" saviours really is.

We have seen that everything revolves around the Trinitarian Father, Son and Spirit who have made all things. They have made us in their image yet we have all—universally, across the world—rebelled against him. We see the evidence of a global rebellion in the global nature of pain and suffering. And so all of this supports the Bible's own teaching that there is one Messiah and he is the Messiah for all sorts of people.

Yes, God revealed that he would work out his plan of redemption through one particular nation: the nation of Israel. Yet his plan was always for redemption to be for all the nations! In Genesis 12:2–3 we read, *"I will make you into a great nation and I will bless you; I will make your name great, and you will be a blessing. I will bless those who bless you, and whoever curses you I will curse; and all peoples on earth will be blessed through you."*

> **Our God is not parochial, nor is he nationalistic.**

Our God is not parochial, nor is he nationalistic. And the great evidence of this was shown on the day of Pentecost when, for the first time since the tower of Babel in Genesis 11, God's name was praised in a wide variety of languages. Why? To signal that now the great news of Jesus Christ was to be taken (and believed upon) by all sorts of people! Our God always had a plan for all the nations of the earth.

What does this teach us? That all people—regardless of the colour of their skin, the tradition of their culture, where they grew up, what they already know of Jesus—they are ALL included in the great invitation to come to Jesus Christ and be saved.

God is not more interested in Jews than Gentiles. We shouldn't have a fixation on "God's plan for the Jews" above his plan for all people. We live *after* Jesus has come. God is not more interested in white people over other people. The historically flawed idea that Christianity is "a white man's religion" is to be rejected. After all, Jesus was a Jew not Anglo-Saxon! And the early church had people from many nations.

And so as you study at university you need to resist the notion that "your beliefs" are just limited. No! What the Bible teaches it teaches to us all; and that means that the solutions for all problems are all to be derived from the book the God of all people has given.

Yes, there will be certain local cultural differences and different emphases for different contexts. But the core principles that govern your studies will still centre on the unifying fact that Jesus Christ is the deepest answer to all mankind's struggles.

3. Christ will eventually "save the planet"

We considered earlier the growing concern about environmental crises. Whilst we need to avoid much human over-confidence in our ability to save things, we Christians must be clear that Jesus Christ will eventually put all things right.

And, again, we can see how a biblical worldview is internally coherent. Yes, the world is messed up, yet that is because God himself has cursed the world due to mankind's sin. Yet there is a redemption for the earth as well. The apostle Paul wrote of it in Romans 8:19–21, *"The creation waits in eager expectation for the sons of God to be revealed. For the creation was subjected to frustration, not by its own choice, but by the will of the one who subjected it, in hope that the creation itself will be liberated from its bondage to decay and brought into the glorious freedom of the children of God."*

One day Jesus will come again and then he will launch

a new heaven and a new earth. The earth will have no curse—it will be Paradise!

Now this biblical worldview is important to understand. Many of you will study material relating to environmental concerns. How optimistic can you be? Are we doomed to an environmental apocalypse? Well, no we aren't. We can be confident that the Lord will maintain life on earth in order to fulfil his purposes and for there to be many of his people around to meet the Lord when he comes. Will the planet then be utterly destroyed? Well, although we cannot be certain of the exact mechanisms he will use, we can be certain that all of creation will be liberated from its bondage to decay.

Should you be passionate about good environmental stewardship? Absolutely. Is it good to study and research ways of limiting environmental damage? Yes: we are to treat all God's world with dignity. But are we the ones who will save the planet? No! We must see hubris for what it is. We are far too weak. Yet, be rock solid in your confidence that eventually Christ will "save the planet".

So, I have taken you on an extended worldview journey in the hope that this will encourage and strengthen your faith. There is only one world and so only one true worldview. The Bible's worldview is not only internally coherent, it also matches well with the experience you and I have of the world.

But these matters are very complex. I have brushed over much and omitted much more. Your challenge is to study and think deeply beyond what I have written. Please do so and use the reading list below to help.

FURTHER READING

Andrews, Edgar, *Who made God?* Darlington, Evangelical Press, 2012.

Ashton, John, *In Six Days.* Green Forest, Master Books, 2007.

Beisner, E Calvin, *Where garden meets wilderness.* Grand Rapids, Eerdmans, 1998.

Burgess, S C, *Hallmarks of Design.* Leominster, DayOne Publications, 2008.

Dembski, William A, *The design of life.* Dallas, Foundation for Thought & Ethics, 2007.

Finlay, Lloyd, Pattemore & Swift, *Debating Darwin.* Milton Keynes, Paternoster, 2009.

Honeysett, Marcus, *Meltdown.* Nottingham, IVP, 2002.

Lennox, John, *God's Undertaker.* Oxford, Lion Books, 2009.

Levin, Norman (ed), *Should Christians Embrace Evolution?* Nottingham, IVP, 2009.

Mangalwadi, Vishal, *The book that made your world.* Nashville, Thomas Nelson, 2011.

Morris, John, *Footprints in the ash.* Green Forest, Master Books, 2003.

Nash, Ronald H, *Worldviews in conflict.* Grand Rapids, Zondervan, 2010.

Noebel, David A, *Understanding the times.* Manitou Springs, Summit Ministries, 1995.

Pearcey, Nancy, *Total Truth.* Wheaton, Crossway, 2008.

Pratt Jr, Richard, *Every Thought Captive.* Phillipsburg, P&R, 2012.

Robertson, David, *The Dawkins Letters.* Fearn, Christian Focus, 2010.

Schmidt, Alvin J, *How Christianity changed the world.* Grand Rapids, Zondervan, 2004.

Sire, James, *The Universe Next Door.* Nottingham, IVP, 2010.

Stark, Rodney, *For the glory of God.* Princeton, Princeton University Press, 2003.

Sproul, R C, *Not a chance.* Grand Rapids, Baker Academic, 1999.

Williams, Peter S, *A sceptic's guide to atheism.* Milton Keynes, Paternoster, 2009.

STUDY QUESTIONS
Part 3: Studying for Christ

1. There is a real danger that being a university student can become your identity. Is this true? What warning signs would you see if this was happening to someone?

2. What practical steps can you take to ensure your healthy desire for hard work does not morph into an unhealthy obsession to achieve?

3. Why must the Bible be every Christian's "Mount Everest" organising text? How does this help us better engage with other books and materials?

4. Why is it important to uphold the Bible's supernatural content?

5. What is the flaw in the analogy that we are all "blind men describing an elephant" when it comes to describing truth?

6. Outline some of the unchallenged assumptions of the naturalist/evolutionary worldview.

PART 4: Witnessing for Christ

BE CREDIBLE

Universities are full of unbelievers and thus share a great deal of the realities of the wider world. Whilst universities are "unreal" in some ways (where else do people have five months off from a full-time occupation?) they are certainly real in terms of their domination by unbelievers. Yet university, having unbelievers with huge amounts of time to think and question the big issues of life, is an ideal place both for formal mission and informal personal evangelism.

But you will only be able to do this if your life is a credible testimony for Christ. No, it will not be in any way perfect but it simply must be credible. After all, if you are openly living contrary to the gospel why should anyone stop to listen to you?

Many students you live and study with will be cynical about religion. To many the hypocrisy of the wider church merges into an assumption of hypocrisy in us all. And of course, none of us is entirely free from hypocrisy! Hypocrisy is having a private life that contradicts our public life. Ouch.

You and I must be seen to be radically different if we are to have credibility. But how? Well, firstly by praying for the Holy Spirit to work holiness in us. Do re-read Chapter 2 of this book. But another way in which we display credibility is by responding in a Christ-like way to our struggles.

We get sick and go to hospital; we have family

troubles; we work hard and don't always achieve the outcome we hoped for; we face many disappointments. But as Christians, as those depending on Christ and his Spirit at work in us, we are able to respond differently. We will not be full of anger, or bitterness, or envy. We will not be full of fear, or doom, or worthlessness. We can look to the Lord and remember all his goodness and promises to help us. And when the folks around us see that we really do trust him, then we will have a credible opportunity to witness.

FURTHER READING:

Barrs, Jerram, *The heart of evangelism*. Nottingham, IVP, 2001.
Dever, Mark, *The Gospel and Personal Evangelism*. Wheaton, Crossway, 2007.

WISELY CONTEXTUALISE

At university you are likely to have opportunities to witness to three fundamentally different types of people:

1. Neutral unbelievers who just want to find out what it is all about

2. Religious unbelievers who hold other views yet want to debate the differences with Christianity

3. Ambivalent unbelievers who don't really believe anything (so they say) yet do have big questions about life

There are probably better ways of classifying people but I suggest everyone is covered by one of these three. I have not included those students who are openly hostile to the Christian faith and refuse to listen as Jesus taught his disciples not to waste time on such people (see Matthew 10v14). But how do you reach these people above, what approaches can you take?

Clearly your goal will be to evangelise: that is, to speak of the Lord Jesus Christ to an unbeliever who is listening. You need an unbeliever; you need an unbeliever who is listening; and you need to speak the gospel message of Christ as Lord and Saviour.

However, you may not be able to start evangelising straightaway. You may need to "do outreach" which is essentially bridge-building to get in contact with unbelievers. You may also need to "do apologetics" which is essentially demolishing wrong thinking so that there is space to build right thinking.

And contextualisation is simply the approach of adapting your starting position to better connect with the person you are seeking to speak to. Let me be clear: everyone has to come to a full understanding of Christ's atoning work on the Cross and how that is the basis for forgiveness. But few conversations can go directly to that after a few minutes. Instead you will need to pray and wisely judge "where people are at" to find a point of genuine contact. Remember how patient Jesus was with his disciples; remember how he went and spent time with them in order to reveal his truth. We must follow our master's approach. Contextualisation then means that you need to consider the person first and slowly bring them to hear the full message of the gospel of Jesus Christ. Here are three contexts you are likely to face at university:

1. NEUTRAL UNBELIEVERS

In many ways students we meet who are peaceful and open to hear our message are the easiest for us to cope with. This means we can probably make the quickest progress in getting to the heart of evangelism: teaching directly from the scriptures. The apostle Paul clearly teaches that someone can be saved ultimately only by hearing the word of God (Romans 10:12–15). This is an important point because some other Christians you meet will suggest that we should used modern alternatives to get our message across. Their argument goes that just as books are old fashioned but films all the rage, so the Bible is less useful than film and drama.

This is undoubtedly true for many things, yet we are to follow God's ways and not our own. Watching a film about Jesus is not wrong but it must never replace God's Word. So if you have the opportunity to use it, then don't miss your chance. Your words spoken from the Bible might well be the method God uses to bring his salvation to someone.

In preparation, you could advertise a series of short talks for a bigger group as a CU event or short Bible studies for one or two people as a private event in hall. The study given by www.christianbasics.org could be a starting template. The important thing with this approach is to go only as fast as the hearers are able to go. Pray before each event that God will use the teaching and resulting discussion to reveal his truth. Carefully but firmly keep the discussion on the main subject at hand. It is all too easy to get side tracked down blind alleys that generate a great deal of heat but little light.

2. RELIGIOUS UNBELIEVERS

Perhaps the greatest surprise you will have is when you talk to people who follow other religions. They may follow a religion you know a little about like Islam or Judaism. Or they may follow a less well known religion like Hinduism, Sikhism, or Zoroastrianism. You are also likely to meet people who are Jehovah's Witnesses, Seventh Day Adventists, Mormons or Quakers. How on earth do you witness to any of these?

Well we can learn again from the example Jesus gave us when he spoke to the Jewish believers in his day.

When Jesus spoke to the Pharisees he always referred to what they believed and then compared this to the true Old Testament scriptures (see Matthew 15:1–20). It is true to say Jesus did at times condemn the Pharisee's actions (like the money changing in the temple in Matthew 21:12–14). However, his main approach was to deal with their teaching and to compare this to his truth.

This approach is better when witnessing to people from other religions. If we try to attack the wrong done by people who follow their religion (like wars, persecution and violence) this not only causes unhelpful offence, but leads the discussion away from the gospel. Also, it can leave us exposed to counter-claims of wrong done in the name of Christianity. Rather than attack or debate behaviour, we ought to focus on their teaching. Where does their holy book come from? Does God claim to be its author and does it stand up to cross-checking? What does it say about God? How does it explain sin and trouble in the world? What is its answer and is it either reliable or possible? None of these questions will guarantee easy answers, but they will help you to focus the discussion on the important issues. God's Word is reliable and certain, and it is unique in teaching that it is God himself who provides salvation and that his salvation is complete and guaranteed to work.

Witnessing to believers from other religions needs to be done with care and respect. Where you can, accommodate their cultural and legitimate preferences. Paul said that he became like Jews to win Jews and like others to win them (see 1 Corinthians 9:19–23). Do some research on the main teachings of these other religions so that you can show an interest. Be willing to find out what they do believe and ask careful

> **Witnessing to believers from other religions needs to be done with care and respect.**

but direct questions where the teaching falls short of the truth. If you engage your friends on matters of truth, you not only avoid offence, but you increase the opportunity to speak of Christ.

3. AMBIVALENT UNBELIEVERS

Perhaps the biggest grouping of students you will have opportunities to reach are those who just wander through life not really thinking about religion. They have probably discounted it as old-fashioned or boring yet they still have many big unanswered questions. Here you will need to put questions in their minds that make them doubt their current assumptions and be more willing to hear what the Bible teaches.

When the apostle Paul was in Athens waiting for his fellow workers to arrive, he saw a city full of people claiming to be wise yet acting foolishly. The Athenians loved thinking and debating how to live, but at the same time were steeped in idolatry. Their idols were not conceptual like those people worship today; they were physical lumps of wood or stone! And so faced with this situation of ambivalent unbelievers who didn't know the first thing about the true God or the Bible, Paul shows wise flexibility in changing his model for preaching. Instead of speaking directly from the scriptures, he assessed the best theme to follow and then presented an entirely scriptural argument but using their own language and culture.

You can read the whole account in Acts 17:16–34. He saw an inscription to "an unknown god" and used this as a starting point to introduce the God who created them and to show that if God is great then how can he be squashed into a lump of stone? If we are like God then how foolish it was to think that a stone was like us! And once he had caught their attention and opened the holes in their argument, he skilfully presented Christ and his resurrection to show how the real God had demonstrated his power and his authority to judge them.

So, in application, you can legitimately follow Paul's approach when your audience or individual friend clearly has no knowledge of the Bible or any real interest in seeking God.

At university you will have many wonderful opportunities to witness and speak about Christ. Make it your aim to use these opportunities wisely. It will take time to carefully demolish false ideas. Go prepared with different strategies for different people. Get involved in your CU and influence it for good. You may want to promote and develop these ideas to produce materials and activities that target these people. The apostle Paul was wise, flexible and above all always focussed on preaching Christ. Sometimes he could speak directly, other times indirectly. You have a wonderful opportunity to bring many more people into God's marvellous light!

FURTHER READING:

Koukl, Greg, *Tactics*. Grand Rapids, Zondervan, 2009.
Metzger, Will, *Tell the Truth*. Nottingham, IVP, 2013.
Newman, Randy, *Questioning Evangelism*. Grand Rapids, Zondervan, 2000.
Stiles, J Mack, *Speaking of Jesus*. Nottingham, IVP, 1995.

PROCLAIM CHRIST

In witnessing for Christ we all face a very real danger of not actually getting to proclaiming Christ himself as the one we must believe and receive by faith. Instead we can easily find ourselves tied up with explaining the logic of the gospel (defending it against claims it cannot be true). We have already spent time in this book considering what makes up a biblical worldview and we have also considered some contextual approaches to engaging with unbelievers. All well and good; but we must pray that we also get beyond these things. It may be helpful to see these as ground clearing exercises—making some space for the truths of Christ.

Perhaps more dangerous is merely explaining the benefits of the gospel such as the blessings that Christians enjoy but not Christ himself. In fact this is more common than you might think. Even some evangelical Christians can unwittingly preach the gospel as if it is merely the means to our own personal happiness. You feel lonely; you are looking to get this or that; you feel guilty. Then the danger is just to treat Christ as a glorious Father Christmas who meets all our needs merely to help us "regroup" and go on living for ourselves! Sadly there are confessing Christians who have this fundamentally selfish understanding of the gospel.

Christ himself was aware of this danger during his earthly ministry. In John 6—the chapter famous for recording his feeding of well over 5,000 people—he explained that the very real blessings of the gospel (forgiveness, peace, assurance, new life, purpose, etc) are actually secondary to the supreme blessing: knowing and having Christ himself.

Jesus could see that most of the crowd of people that followed him after the miracle had got the wrong end of the stick. They followed him because the prospect of free food was clearly very appealing.

And the following day Jesus made a blunt assessment: *"Jesus answered them, 'Truly, truly, I say to you, you are seeking me, not because you saw signs, but because you ate your fill of the loaves. Do not work for the food that perishes, but for the food that endures to eternal life, which the Son of Man will give to you. For on him God the Father has set his seal'"* (John 6:26).

The crowd wanted a "new Moses" to feed them new bread (like the ultimate UN Food Programme!). But in v49–50 Jesus explained, *"Your fathers ate the manna in the wilderness, and they died. This is the bread that comes down from heaven, so that one may eat of it and not die."* Jesus wanted to show them that he hadn't come merely to give physical blessings but spiritual bread! And what was that bread? He explained in v48, *"I am the bread of life."*

The point Jesus was making was that he does not merely provide the "bread of life" (as if it was something outside of himself that we can receive a helping of). Rather he was teaching that he *himself* is the bread of life.

And so the heart of evangelism is proclaiming that it

is believing and receiving Christ himself that forms the heart of the gospel message. Or as Jesus put it in verse 40, *"look on the Son and believe."*

Jesus *himself* is God's great gift; he *himself* is spiritual life. And from having him—described as the bread of life—then we really do receive all the benefits we have already mentioned.

Why am I labouring this point? Because the sinfulness of sin means that it is possible to be guilty of "asset stripping Christ" for what we can get from him, rather than treasuring and loving and having him for all that he is in himself: the eternal Son of the eternal Father given to us to enjoy deep fellowship and personal relationship. Jesus himself is who we must have.

Authentic love is for the person not their possessions; authentic love sees the day-by-day relationship as the most treasured thing. And authentic love for Jesus is the same. How terrible it would be for someone to claim to love Jesus when in fact they merely love themselves. We must be careful therefore to proclaim Christ as the pearl of greatest price, and not merely his blessings.

FUTURE READING:

Chapell, Bryan, *Christ Centred Preaching.* Grand Rapids, Baker Academic, 2005.
Dickson, John, *Simply Christianity.* Sydney, Matthias Media, 1999.

UNITE CAREFULLY

At university you will quickly learn that not all who call themselves Christians believe or practice what you do. It is a sad reality that over the last two thousand years of church history there have been (and still are) a bewilderingly large variety of biblical interpretations and behaviour. As a young Christian you will need to be prepared for this. Not only will other Christians question and debate with you, but non-Christians will either assume we are all the same or attack us for our disunity. Dealing with difference within the wider Christian church is not easy. And so you do need to be prepared before you arrive. There are three essential biblical principles that we will look at to help us cope with this issue.

1. THE BIBLE IS OUR BASIS

Our starting point must always be that the Bible is God's inspired and faultless Word such that it is our main and final source of truth. The Puritan Christians had a Latin phrase '*Sola Scriptura*' which means 'Scripture Alone'. This sums up this principle. The apostle Paul teaches us in 2 Timothy 3:16 that *"All scripture is breathed out by God and profitable for teaching, for reproof, for correction and for training in righteousness, that the man of God may be competent, equipped for every good work."*

If our starting and ending points are scripture then we have the best hope that we will reach the truth and thus come to unity. Yes, there are textual issues and difficulties with some passages. Yet almost all biblical scholars who have the highest regard and submission to scripture agree over a great deal of biblical text. No, reading the Bible will not automatically sweep away all the differences but it is and must be the starting point if agreement is ever to be made. The way we are to deal with the difficult passages is to use the easier ones as lights to shine their truths onto these more difficult ones. We know that the Bible cannot contradict itself because it is written by a God who cannot lie.

When Jesus taught his disciples he often used Old Testament scriptures to drive home his point. He knew that all that had been written was in agreement with what he was saying. An example of this is his so-called Sermon on the Mount recorded in Matthew 5:1–48. When the apostle Paul was defending the gospel against Jewish opposition he always used the Old Testament scriptures (also see Acts 13:16–44 and Acts 17:2). Paul's authority and basis for his teaching was God's Word. This model of teaching and reasoning is the one we should follow. As a student attempting to debate and talk with other Christians, you should derive and defend your beliefs from the Bible. If you cannot do this and they can then they might be right!

2. SPEAK THE TRUTH IN LOVE

When Paul taught the Ephesians why they had been given elders, one of the reasons he gives is that the people will be equipped to speak *"the truth in love"*

(Ephesians 4:15). Sadly our first principle of Sola Scriptura is often taken without this equally important one of love. In teaching the Corinthians, Paul famously said that if we do not have love we are like *"a noisy gong or a clanging cymbal"* (1 Corinthians 13:1). We need to constantly remind ourselves that whatever light we have from the scriptures we have by God's grace which has come to us from the Holy Spirit (1 Corinthians 2:14–16).

Most evangelicals rightly stand firm on the centrality of scripture. However they do also seem to have a reputation for arguing their case without much love and care. Yet to win the argument in an unloving way is dishonouring to the Lord. If we claim to live by the Spirit then we should display his fruit. We will have (amongst other qualities) patience and self-control (see Galatians 5:25). And yet the greatest of these is love. Someone once said that we can often be quick to teach the importance of the doctrines of grace yet too slow to show the grace that should come from knowing these doctrines. As you engage in lively and spirited debate with other Christians at university, always do so with love.

3. LEAVE ROOM FOR CONSCIENCE

God has wisely given Christians a certain amount of freedom of individual conscience. This should not be stretched to allow personal interpretation to rule the day, but neither should it be squashed so that it cannot be applied to the minor matters where cultural differences are likely. In 1 Corinthians 10:23–33, the apostle Paul outlined this principle in the context of eating meat offered to idols. Paul's argument was that whilst meat is just meat and idols are powerless, nevertheless we should respect another person's conscience if *he is* worried about eating such meat. Although there may be no absolute wrong in this case we should seek the good of the other person and not violate his conscience.

Now of course this isn't easy in practice because the argument continues over what is a "conscience matter"! One person's matter of conscience may be another person's down-the-line essential biblical teaching. On some matters of detail it may be better to leave a difference for the sake of unity and fellowship rather than squeeze every last drop of conformity. How can we decide this? Well, remember again that James teaches us that *"if any of you lacks wisdom, let him ask God"* (James 1:5).

> The aim in speaking with your brother or sister should be their growth in grace.

By way of application then to students, the aim in speaking with your brother or sister should be their growth in grace. If they are new believers, do not burden them with issues that they cannot yet be expected to understand. Some people will have entirely different church backgrounds and you should exercise patience to judge when (if ever) it is appropriate for you to start or continue a debate on a particular issue. It is all too easy just to aim at winning an argument or even (sadly) to show superior biblical knowledge rather than to aim to build the other person up. As an undergraduate from a very conservative background I sadly enjoyed quoting from this and that passage more than listening to the real needs of my friends.

You should also avoid discussions that are like, as Jesus put it, *"straining out a gnat and swallowing a camel!"* (Matthew 23:24). Too much attention can easily be spent on minor issues when there are either major issues that do need to be debated or that are already agreed on! Whilst as individual Christians you may end up attending different churches (quite rightly) because of differences, these differences may not need to divide and thus spoil your fellowship at other times.

However, having made the point for encouraging agreement and fellowship where appropriate you do also need to watch out for serious error that might do you real harm. The apostle Peter warns us about such "false teachers" that can lead us to ruin (See 2 Peter 2:1–22). Universities are sometimes breeding grounds for cults and single-issue sects and so you need to be able to discern between false and true teachers. Even spending lots of social time with such people can be dangerous. When I was an undergraduate, a group teaching that baptism was essential for salvation caused a great deal of trouble and even led to a ban on all religious groups in the student hall where I lived. Whilst no single test is likely to discern all issues, a good starting question to "see where a person is" might be to ask what they are depending on to get to heaven. If the person doesn't clearly point to the finished work of Christ alone given to them entirely by God's grace, then you will have fundamental differences and need to tread carefully. Another helpful guide someone gave to me was the four major aspects of true Christianity:

1. Accepting the sufficiency and authority of scripture
2. Believing the centrality and vitality of the cross
3. Having an ongoing personal relationship with God
4. Submitting to the Lordship of Christ

If you can make friends with other students who believe these fundamental truths, they are likely to do you good and you will have good fellowship. Students who do not hold these views may well be Christians (albeit poorly taught). The Lord doesn't want you to bash them to pieces by exposing their mistakes. Rather, he wants you to demonstrate God's grace in you by building them up in their faith (Romans 15:1–6).

But perhaps the most important preparation you need is practical experience in the art of handling the scriptures. Whilst you won't have all the answers at your fingertips, you can help cope with your many student discussions by going to university with a good grounding in how to study the Bible. You need to know the fundamentals of the faith and I recommend www. christianbasics.org as one such study course to follow.

You could use this as a guide to teaching others whom you meet. As well as knowing the fundamentals in your head, you need to know how to reason them from the scriptures. If you cannot do this for the easier subjects, you will have no hope with the trickier "hot topics". Study God's Word now so that it is not an unfamiliar book to you when someone asks you a question. How would you go about teaching someone about God's sovereignty? Where would you turn to show that Jesus is the exclusive way to God?

Finally, do not regard difference as something to be avoided at all costs. Whilst you must agree with others on the fundamentals of the faith to have any meaningful fellowship, Christian debate can and should be a good thing. Not only will it strengthen your understanding of what you do believe and sift out your misunderstandings, it will also encourage you as you see that the Bible does stand up to close scrutiny. You should have no "no-go" areas; by debating with others you will see that God's truth is both consistent and credible!

FUTURE READING:

Lane, Tim & Paul Tripp, *Relationships, a mess worth making.*
    Darlington, Evangelical Press, 2010.
Milne, Bruce, *Know the truth.* Nottingham, IVP, 2009.
Sande, Ken, *The Peacemaker.* Grand Rapids, Baker Books, 2004.

STUDY QUESTIONS
Part 4: Witnessing for Christ

1. What is hypocrisy? Why is this such a fatal thing? Can any of us be totally free from it?

2. Why is it important to contextualise in order to witness to unbelievers? What is the danger if this goes too far?

3. What approaches are more likely to be productive when engaging with people already holding to established religious views?

4. Why is it so important that we bring people to hear and learn about Jesus Christ?

5. What basic framework are we wise to use when considering whether to join with other Christian groups?

6. What is it to speak the truth in love? Why is this so hard and so rarely seen?

PART 5: After you've been

REMEMBER YOUR ROOTS

Going to university is often a tremendously exciting and fulfilling experience. Friendships are made for life, perspectives and understanding on wider cultural and social ideas are expanded, and lasting tools for learning and self development are secured. But as you contemplate leaving the university scene can I urge you to embrace the wider world as well?

Some of you will change dramatically over the three or more years you are at university. Some of you might continue with postgraduate studies and so be "at university" for a considerable time. Yet can I urge you to remember all the people who you have known outside of your studies as well? Three or more years when you are young make a big difference. The idea of "going to live back at home" may be difficult. But please do not forget your family and your childhood friends. Sadly some students at certain universities learn how to "redefine" themselves socially away from their childhood past. Of course, you may well change a lot but as a Christian you must be careful not to allow social or economic barriers to develop.

There is, after all, a reasonably high chance that you will get a graduate job and probably therefore enjoy (in the longer term) financial benefits too. You are also more likely to marry a graduate as often romantic relationships blossom at university. You are also more likely to settle in the area where you studied than back in your home location. And therefore you need to work hard to maintain good links and genuine relationships with your family and friends back home. I sadly know of one student who largely disowned his working class provincial family as he redefined himself as a metropolitan styled lawyer. How sad and how unkind to all those who served him sacrificially for years to give him his opportunity to study.

Some of you will be the first people from your families to go to university. Some of you will be the first people from your home area or local community. Can I urge you not to reject your roots and allow university to redefine you in the wrong way?

For many Christians (and therefore local churches) social class unity proves a much harder reality than racial unity. If you allow your identity to be shaped more by your studies than by being in Christ you will follow the world's preference to be ever more "upwardly mobile". Just as your studies can wrongly become your identity, so can your career and professional profile. You need to strive hard (and pray often) to maintain a unity with a wide group of Christian brothers and sisters and certainly not just graduates!

Perhaps you should seriously consider going back to your home church and location in order to help where few others are willing to be? Perhaps you should consider your social or racial roots as an opportunity to live for Christ and share the many blessings you have received from your university studies?

LIVE TO SERVE

Wherever you end up (and I realise a whole pile of factors will affect that) can I urge you to maintain much of the momentum you have hopefully gained away at university? Often the hard work and disciplined study patterns you have made can help you be a great help in the life of your local church or wider community. Beyond your studies I want you to see one thing as all important: the life of service. Serving others in the body of Christ is the hallmark of a healthy Christian life. It is the practical application of being "like Christ".

As you transition from your studies you will face the pressure to be consumed by your new career. In addition, the wonderful developments in your personal life (perhaps marriage and children!) can become overwhelming distractions from a commitment to the life of your local church.

Don't let this happen! Keep up the momentum you have gained at university in your active service for Christ and his interests. You need to continue to live to serve him.

Just before he laid down his life for them, Jesus taught his disciples that service was at the heart of being one of his followers. He did this through the visual demonstration of washing their feet. By that selfless, counter-cultural act of service he was making a significant point. But had they fully understood?

We read in John 13:12, "*When he had washed their feet and put on his outer garments and resumed his place, he said to them, 'Do you understand what I have done to you?'*" Jesus wasn't doubting their ability to see, nor their ability to feel, nor even their ability to understand the physical act of washing their feet. But he doubted their ability to truly understand what he had done—and what that meant for them.

And so, after testing whether they really wanted to be taught by him and whether they really wanted to obey him, he gave them his sermon punchline in verse 17: "*If you know these things, blessed are you if you do them.*" Merely knowing about service is not enough. You will only find the blessing if you actually live to serve!

And this is a paradox because the assumed truth we all have by default is this: we will be happy when we get what we want, when we are the centre of attention, and people serve us. That is the global, working assumption all of us have from birth. Why? Because that is the principle that the devious master called Sin whispers in our ears.

> **Real happiness comes from serving others!**

Yet Jesus teaches the service paradox: real happiness comes from serving others! And so you need to hold on to this paradoxical truth beyond your studies. The Lord has not given you time at university merely to better yourself and climb the ladder of your career. He has not given you these opportunities just so you can live wholly for yourself and your new family. No, you are to use all the benefits and lessons you have learned for the service of others. You are to use the gifts and abilities you have to help your brothers and sisters in Christ.

After all, wasn't that exactly what Jesus did? That is why he said, *"For even the Son of Man came not to be served but to serve, and to give his life as a ransom for many."* (Mark 10:45). And that is why he also said, *"If anyone would come after me, let him deny himself and take up his cross and follow me"* (Mark 8:34).

Jesus——the supreme example of humanity——served his Father's will above his own; and loved his disciples by serving them. And yet was astonishingly full of joy even in the hardest situations! That is the service paradox!

And that is what you are called to do after you leave university. Don't use all your advantages simply for personal success. Be bright——shine for Christ——and live to serve.

FURTHER READING:

Harris, Alex & Brett, *Do Hard Things*. Colorado Springs, Multnomah, 2008.

Stott, John, *The Radical Disciple*. Leicester, IVP, 2010.

STUDY QUESTIONS
Part 5: After you've been

1. In what ways might going to university tempt you to distance yourself from your childhood roots? Why would this matter?

2. For many Christians social class barriers prove harder to remove than race barriers. Why is this, and what can you do to remove the barrier of class?

3. What other challenges do you expect new graduates to face as they transition into life beyond university?

4. Jesus teaches the service paradox: real happiness comes from serving others! Why is this? How can you best organise your graduate life in order to serve others?

5. Discuss the ways in which your university days might help to encourage and strengthen the life of the local church you join after graduation?

6. Looking to the rest of your life, what big plans do you have for serving Christ and his people?

APPENDIX: WHY GO?

Clearly whether you should go to university or not depends on your own personal circumstances. But it is important that you think it through so you can make the wisest decision.

In the 1960s, around 5% of school leavers went to university in the UK. Since then, both the number of universities and the places they offer has dramatically increased. By 2002 the proportion had risen to around 35% and in 2014 a record 49% are expected to experience some form of Higher Education. And so, with many more places now on offer, it will be easier for you to get accepted on a university course somewhere. Many people today will tell you that you really do need to go because most jobs require "graduate skills". So don't be surprised if the teachers at your school or college urge you to go.

So what are the biblical principles you should apply in testing whether it is wise for you to go? Well, please consider the following three:

1. CONTENTMENT

God calls you to be content in whatever walk of life he gives you. The apostle Paul tells us *"there is great gain in godliness with contentment"* (see 1 Timothy 6:6). Not everyone is suited for university. After all, it is intended to be a place of academic study and not everyone is cut out for that. Nor does everyone need to go to university. There are plenty of worthwhile jobs and careers that do not and will not require graduate skills. And so the first thing you need to do is to ask yourself whether you have the academic ability and the real need to go?

In the Bible we can see that God has saved people to serve him from a wide variety of backgrounds. The apostle Paul came from a more academic background and had been taught by Gamaliel who was a doctor of the Pharisee's law and one of the most revered teachers of his time (see Acts 5:34 and Acts 22:3). Today Paul would have probably gone to university and ended up with a Doctor of Divinity degree. We know God used him mightily in preaching the gospel using his razor-sharp logic to confront the great philosophers of his time (see Acts 17:16–34). And yet in contrast to Paul, God also called the apostle Peter who came from a more vocational background. Peter was a fisherman (see Matthew 4:18) and today he would probably have left school at sixteen and learnt his trade from others whilst earning a wage. God used him mightily in preaching the gospel, particularly on the Day of Pentecost (see Acts 2:14) and also to go on to write warm pastoral letters to Christians facing hardship and persecution (see 1 & 2 Peter). So we can see from just these two examples that education was in no way a barrier to serving God. In fact God puts his people in all walks of life so that all sorts of people can be reached.

Unfortunately there has long been a view that the "professions" are more important than the "trades" with the idea that people with degrees are more valuable. But we have already seen that God certainly doesn't think like this. Peter was used to preach perhaps the most dramatic sermon of all time that launched the New Testament church! Perhaps the most compelling example is Jesus himself who chose a career as a carpenter before his ministry began (see Mark 6:3). There is absolutely nothing undignified or second-rate about a non-university career. Remember that pleasing God is far more important than keeping in with your school friends.

Another great change over the last 30 years has been the opportunities for part-time university studies. No longer is the option between full time and not going. Many students have the opportunities to study while they work so they can both afford it and test out whether it is right for them. In addition, mature student opportunities are now available for those who didn't go to university when they left school, but wish to after a few years at work. These changes reduce the pressure of going straight after leaving school. In a very real sense, opportunities now exist to go later on in life.

If academic study is something you don't enjoy or if the career you want to follow clearly does not need a degree, then think twice before deciding to go to university. God calls you to be content with the skills and interests he has given to you. Whether he is calling you to be a theologian, a fisherman or anything else, if you are a Christian you can be sure he has good works planned specifically for you (see Ephesians 2:10).

2. REALISM

In deciding whether to go to university, you need to sit down and "count the cost" both in time and money. Are you prepared to stick at your studies and keep going to the end? You may well have the abilities needed for university and a degree may well help you in your career, but are you prepared to do what it takes for the next three to five years of your life? Some people start university in the autumn full of enthusiasm but soon begin to weary when the reality of hard work and long periods of study begin to bite! For some, the prospect of returning after the Christmas vacation is too much, and they drop out.

When Jesus was teaching his followers about the cost of being a disciple he taught an important principle. In Luke 14:25–34 Jesus confronted the issue of perseverance. He used a simple illustration. Suppose someone is about to build a tower. Well you'd expect that before launching straight into the action, he or she would first sit down and work out the cost and effort for the whole project. How long would it take? How many people will be needed to do the work? How much material, bricks and cement? What is the estimated total cost? After considering all these things, the person would then decide whether or not to go ahead.

Just imagine the embarrassment if he didn't count the cost at the start! The foundations are laid, the local newspaper has shown the artist's impression of the final tower, everyone is eagerly looking on ...

but the builder then announces that he has run out of money. He hasn't got enough to go further than the foundations! Why, people would laugh. They would certainly think the man foolish not to have planned ahead. And his chances of getting a job building another tower would be pretty low. No, we would rather expect the person to have sat down and thought it through. He or she would have saved up or secured a loan, employed the right people and planned out a work schedule to get the full tower built.

> Before deciding to go to university, you need to count the full cost of what lies ahead.

Now Jesus used this illustration to show that Christians need to count the cost of following him. But the principle is a wider one that we can apply here. Before deciding to go to university, you need to count the full cost of what lies ahead. What do I mean? Well here are two things to consider.

a. Hard work

This is what university is about. A degree worth having will require you to attend your lectures and practicals, and to put in at least 3 evenings a week of intense study (I'm assuming a full-time course). The work you will do is designed to be hard, yet if you get accepted on the course that means you have proved you are capable of doing the work. You will have to re-read your notes and read extra material in the library. Are you prepared to do this for each of the years you are at university?

Now, I don't write this to make university seem unbearable! It is true that *"all work and no play makes Jack a dull boy"*. But Jack is meant to be working a lot of the time. Hopefully the subjects you take will interest you such that you will enjoy your time learning and researching. But do count the cost of evenings alone in private study, the discipline of attending lectures and handing work in on time. The students who get to the end and pass are the ones who counted the cost at the start and said "Yes, I'm prepared to put in the effort, all of the time." And in case you're feeling discouraged, the clear majority of students do pass!

b. Less money

Unless you're particularly "well heeled", your years at university will not give you much extra cash. Sadly the days of student grants and bursaries are gone for the majority and so it's more likely that you will live on a low income, and probably supplement this with a loan or part-time job. On the other hand, your friends who choose not to go to university will be proudly spending their first wage and, possibly, buying their first car! Are you prepared to wait a few years before earning a good wage? Do you see your university years as an investment for the future such that you are willing, and content to wait?

Whatever the rights and wrongs of student finance, the reality is that student life requires very tight financial management. Are you prepared to accept this situation? Depending on your location and the type of accommodation you get, your "spending money" might be very tight. And this will be for a number of years. Of course, the career opportunities and the satisfaction from study can more than make up for this temporary hardship. Most graduates do go on to earn far more over their careers to compensate for the few years of hardship. But do be sure that you are willing to put up with it at the time!

3. Honour

The third principle to be considered is that we should only do things that bring honour to God. Is the subject you are thinking of studying one that is suitable for a Christian? Now we must tread carefully here because depending on our starting point, we can reach different conclusions.

The apostle Paul is very clear in teaching us that *"whatever you do, do all to the glory of God"* (see 1 Corinthians 10:31). This demolishes the popular idea that we have two lives: a spiritual one for God and a secular one where we can more or less live like everyone else. This idea was developed around the time of the so-called Enlightenment. Yet whilst it was correct in separating church and state, it is wrongly applied to suggest "Bible-free zones" in our individual lives. Everything we do either honours or dishonours God. Whether it is singing hymns in church or watching television at home. Each of these can bring honour or dishonour.